AI Risks & Safety

Protecting People, Businesses, and Nations in the Age of Intelligent Machines.

Written by
Eric LeBouthillier

AcraSolution | 2025 1st Edition
www.acrasolution.com

Preface

Who This Book Is For

This book is written for **government leaders, business executives, technology professionals, educators, and everyday citizens** who want to better understand both the promise and the dangers of artificial intelligence. Policymakers will find insights into regulation and security, companies will discover strategies to protect their operations and reputations, and home users will gain practical steps to keep themselves and their families safe in a connected world. Whether you are shaping national policy, managing an enterprise, or simply using smart devices at home, this book equips you with the knowledge to stay ahead of the risks.

What You Can Expect

Inside these chapters, you'll uncover the **hidden risks of AI** that often go unnoticed—bias, deepfakes, cyberattacks, privacy invasions, automation pitfalls, and more. You'll also learn about **proven strategies and frameworks** governments, businesses, and individuals can use to protect themselves. Each chapter includes eye-opening examples, real-world case studies, and actionable safeguards you can apply immediately. By the end, you'll not only understand the risks but also gain a **proactive roadmap for building safer, more responsible AI systems** that benefit society instead of endangering it.

Table of Contents

CHAPTER 1

The AI Revolution and Its Hidden Risks

Why AI Is the Most Disruptive Force Since the Internet

AI isn't just another tech trend — it's the first truly general-purpose disruptor since the birth of the internet. While cloud, mobile, and even blockchain made waves in specific sectors, AI is changing the *underlying fabric* of how work gets done across *every* industry. And it's doing it faster, with far less warning.

For SMBs, that's not just fascinating — it's threatening. Not because AI itself is dangerous, but because most organizations are now being **outpaced** by it. It's shifting competitive landscapes, upending customer expectations, rewriting productivity norms, and introducing entirely new categories of risk — *from data exposure to algorithmic liability.*

If the internet connected everything, AI is now interpreting everything. And that changes the rules of the game.

From Digital Plumbing to Cognitive Infrastructure

The internet gave us access. AI gives us cognition. That's the core difference — and the reason AI's impact is broader and more personal.

When the internet emerged, businesses scrambled to "get online" — to launch websites, digitize marketing, and adopt email. It changed how companies connected with customers, vendors, and markets. But AI isn't about connection. It's about *decision-making* — replacing human judgment in ways that can either amplify results or accelerate mistakes at scale.

Here's how that shift plays out in real terms:

- AI drafts emails and legal documents that used to take hours.
- It decides which job candidates get filtered in or out.
- It monitors customer tone and sentiment in real time.
- It auto-generates product descriptions, pricing models, and analytics reports.
- It evaluates network traffic for threats — and sometimes acts on it autonomously.

Each of these are decisions that once relied on human skill. Now they happen at machine speed, often invisibly. The problem? Most SMBs don't realize how fast *delegation to AI* is happening behind the scenes — especially through third-party tools.

AI Moves Faster Than Human Policy

Unlike the internet, which evolved in tandem with regulatory frameworks over decades, AI is outpacing law, governance, and even understanding. There is no "AI manual" SMBs can follow. That's why AI represents not just a technical shift, but an existential one.

You're no longer asking, "How can I use AI to improve operations?" but rather, "Where is AI already making decisions I don't control, and what's the risk if it fails?"

This is a critical inflection point. AI is being baked into CRMs, ERPs, HR platforms, marketing tools, and IT stacks — often by vendors who don't fully disclose what data their models use, how they make decisions, or who owns the outputs.

And unlike the internet, which required human action to publish, post, or transact, AI systems can now act *autonomously* — escalating risks in both speed and scale.

Common Pitfalls in Recognizing AI's Impact

- Believing AI is only relevant to tech companies or large enterprises
- Treating AI as an "add-on" instead of a fundamental workflow change
- Assuming third-party vendors have AI risk fully under control
- Failing to map where AI is already in use across departments

It's Not Just a Tool — It's an Operator

This is where most SMBs underestimate what's changed. AI doesn't just sit in a dashboard waiting for you to prompt it. Increasingly, it operates independently — ingesting data, running logic, and making decisions based on criteria you may not have visibility into.

Think of AI as a new type of employee. Except you didn't interview it. You didn't train it. You don't fully understand what it knows, or how it works. And yet, it's already acting on your behalf — in marketing, customer service, finance, HR, and IT.

That's not a theoretical concern. It's a practical one. If AI produces a misleading report, recommends a biased hiring decision, leaks sensitive client data, or misinterprets regulatory language — *you're liable, not the algorithm.*

Tactical Best Practices

- Audit where AI-powered features exist in your existing tools
- Ask vendors for transparency reports on how AI models work and what data they use
- Establish internal guidelines on acceptable and unacceptable AI use

- Treat AI systems as semi-autonomous operators — assign oversight accordingly
- Train staff to recognize when they are interacting with or relying on AI

Real-World Example: The Legal Bot That Filed a Risky Contract

What Happened

A mid-sized real estate firm adopted an AI-powered document assistant bundled with their contract management software. One day, an account manager used it to draft a lease agreement with custom terms for a large commercial client. The assistant pulled language from prior contracts and public legal templates, then auto-filled key clauses and emailed the contract directly to the client's legal team.

The manager never reviewed the AI's output in detail, assuming it was based on previous templates.

What Went Wrong

The AI had included a non-standard indemnity clause that shifted liability for structural damage onto the client — something the firm never intended. The client flagged the clause, questioned the firm's professionalism, and paused negotiations for weeks.

When the error was discovered, the vendor stated that the AI system "learned" from a previous upload that included a custom contract from a one-off case, and no human had reviewed the logic applied.

What We Learn

Even low-visibility AI tools, when integrated deeply into daily workflows, can create significant business risk. Without clear oversight, AI can amplify edge-case logic, generate misleading outputs, or bypass standard review processes. **Autonomy plus opacity equals risk.**

AI Shrinks the Gap Between Mistake and Consequence

This is the real disruption. AI reduces the time between a bad decision and its consequences. It can send, publish, submit, or delete with no delay — no "are you sure?" prompt that a human might stop and consider.

It also erodes the feedback loop. Traditional mistakes usually generate alerts, tickets, or angry phone calls. But when AI errors are subtle — like tone-deaf marketing copy, biased candidate scoring, or quiet compliance oversights — they may go unnoticed for weeks. Until it's too late.

For SMBs, this means **response time is no longer the buffer it used to be.** You don't have the luxury of catching mistakes downstream. Prevention now lives upstream — in design, oversight, and policy.

The Double-Edged Sword: Innovation vs. Unintended Harm

Artificial intelligence offers a surge of innovation unlike anything we've seen before. Done well, it can save time, boost productivity, reveal insights, and scale operations in ways most SMBs could only dream of a few years ago. But that same power — deployed carelessly or without clear oversight — can cause damage just as fast.

AI doesn't just accelerate what works. It accelerates *whatever it's pointed at.* And when that includes flawed logic, biased data, or hidden gaps in your process, the consequences are magnified at machine scale.

This is the tension at the heart of every AI adoption decision: **How do we benefit from the innovation without opening the door to hidden harm?**

Speed Meets Blind Spots

One of AI's most seductive qualities is speed. It can write, predict, recommend, and execute in seconds. But speed without guardrails is where many SMBs are now getting burned.

When an AI engine processes data or makes recommendations, it doesn't *understand* context — it recognizes patterns and applies probability. That means:

- A customer service AI might escalate a benign complaint into a flagged dispute.
- A hiring assistant might auto-reject qualified candidates based on non-obvious bias.
- A finance tool might flag legitimate expenses as fraud due to outlier data points.
- A chatbot might leak sensitive information it wasn't supposed to access.

None of these are malicious acts. But all of them can damage trust, harm brand perception, or even lead to regulatory consequences — and they usually start from good intentions.

Common Pitfalls That Fuel Unintended Harm

- Deploying AI features without clearly defined boundaries or escalation paths
- Failing to test AI outputs under real-world, high-stakes scenarios
- Believing vendor claims about "safe AI" without validating assumptions
- Assuming that if an AI-generated result *looks good*, it *is* good

Real-World Example: The Marketing AI That Violated Compliance

What Happened

A health-focused SMB used an AI-driven marketing platform to generate and distribute personalized email campaigns. The platform promised better engagement through tailored messaging powered by behavioral data. One campaign targeted patients with messages referencing their recent health conditions — a feature enabled by pulling CRM data through an API integration.

Unfortunately, the campaign violated HIPAA guidelines by including sensitive medical references in public email content.

What Went Wrong

The team assumed the AI would filter out protected health information (PHI) or at least flag sensitive content. But the tool had no awareness of compliance thresholds. It simply used available data to improve engagement metrics — doing exactly what it was designed to do.

The result: multiple complaints, legal reviews, and a temporary shutdown of all outbound communications. The trust damage lingered far longer.

What We Learn

Even well-intended use of AI, when combined with highly regulated data, can produce *outcomes that breach the law.* Innovation was not the problem — the *lack of guardrails* and overconfidence in the system were. SMBs must ensure AI tools are compliance-aware and that *human review isn't optional.*

Innovation Without Supervision Is a Liability

Too many AI deployments go live without a real chain of accountability. Teams think, "It's just a time-saver," or "It's just content generation." But AI systems, even in simple roles, operate based on rules and logic that may not match your values, your policies, or your obligations.

In this way, AI is not just a software feature — it's a decision layer. When you put it into production, you're letting it make calls that affect customers, partners, operations, and compliance. If no one's assigned to *own those decisions,* you're flying blind.

Checklist: How to Balance Innovation with Risk Mitigation

- ☐ Before rollout, test AI outputs against worst-case scenarios
- ☐ Designate internal owners for each AI system's behavior and risk exposure
- ☐ Use tools with transparent logic — or demand explainability from vendors
- ☐ Integrate a human-in-the-loop review process, especially for high-stakes outputs
- ☐ Set clear "fail-safe" conditions — when AI must defer to a human
- ☐ Keep logs and audit trails of AI-driven decisions and communications

Beware of "Good Enough" Automation

Many AI tools prioritize performance metrics over precision. A chatbot trained to deflect calls may succeed by ending 80% of conversations quickly — but if that includes legitimate support requests, you've traded innovation for erosion of trust. A pricing engine that boosts conversion by 5% may be undervaluing your premium offerings or alienating core customers.

Efficiency at the cost of integrity is not a win.

This is where SMBs need to shift their mindset from **"What can this tool do?"** to **"What happens if it goes wrong?"**

AI Is Still Software — But It Behaves Differently

It's easy to assume AI is just "advanced automation." But unlike traditional software, AI systems don't execute fixed commands. They *learn* from data, shift behavior over time, and often generate outputs you didn't explicitly ask for. This makes their behavior more unpredictable — and their failures harder to trace.

In a traditional system, if something breaks, you follow the code. In an AI system, you follow the *data*, the *training process*, and sometimes even the hidden layers of a model you don't own or understand.

That's why the harm often feels surprising, even to experienced teams.

Tactical Best Practices

- Treat all AI systems as non-deterministic: test for edge cases, not just averages
- Monitor for "drift" — when AI behavior changes over time due to new data inputs
- Segment use cases by risk level: marketing copy ≠ financial modeling
- Build approval gates into your workflows for all external-facing AI outputs

Where AI Is Already Shaping Decisions You Don't See

AI isn't just something you *choose* to adopt anymore. In many cases, it's already shaping outcomes inside your business — invisibly, automatically, and often without any explicit approval from leadership. That's the new reality for SMBs: even if you haven't "deployed AI," it's already at work inside your CRM, your marketing stack, your HR tools, and your cybersecurity systems.

The real risk isn't intentional misuse. It's silent delegation. Decisions are being made — about your customers, your data, your hiring, your pricing — without anyone realizing an AI system is behind them.

Invisible AI Is Everywhere

Most modern software platforms now integrate some form of machine learning or AI-driven logic. But they don't always label it clearly. You might see vague features like "smart insights," "automated suggestions," "predictive analytics," or "intelligent optimization" — all euphemisms for algorithms acting on your data.

These aren't just dashboards showing trends. These are decision engines — influencing what your team sees, prioritizes, and acts on.

Here are a few examples of where "invisible AI" is already operating inside many SMB environments:

- **CRM Platforms**: Suggesting which leads are "most likely to close"
- **Email Tools**: Auto-personalizing subject lines or segmenting recipients
- **HR Systems**: Ranking job applicants or flagging "culture fit"
- **Security Suites**: Deciding which alerts to escalate or suppress
- **Finance Apps**: Categorizing expenses and suggesting budget reallocations
- **Customer Support Tools**: Routing tickets or prioritizing inquiries based on sentiment

These decisions might sound helpful — and many of them are — but they're often made without transparency. If the logic is flawed or the training data is biased, *you may never know.*

Common Pitfalls

- Not knowing which features in your tools are powered by AI
- Assuming automated recommendations are neutral or risk-free
- Delegating decisions to software without internal review or override capacity
- Treating AI output as data rather than interpretation

The Dangerous Illusion of Control

Many SMB leaders believe their team is still making all the key decisions. But the moment a system pre-filters information — recommending which leads to call first, which resumes to read, or which transactions look suspicious — *it's already shaping the outcome.*

Humans tend to trust what's surfaced first. That's a known cognitive bias called **algorithmic anchoring** — we give disproportionate weight to the first recommendation we see, especially if it's data-driven or appears "intelligent."

This means your team may be executing AI-shaped decisions without ever questioning the source or logic behind them.

And when something goes wrong — a discriminatory hiring trend, a customer segment that's neglected, a pricing error — you're still accountable, even if the mistake originated in a black-box model you didn't build.

Checklist: How to Identify Hidden AI in Your Stack

- ☐ Review all tools with "smart," "predictive," or "automated" features
- ☐ Ask vendors directly which features use AI or machine learning
- ☐ Document where AI is influencing prioritization, segmentation, or automation
- ☐ Track which business decisions are made by system suggestion vs. human judgment
- ☐ Build override workflows: make it easy for staff to question or bypass AI-driven choices

Real-World Example: The "Smart" Lead Scoring That Cost Sales

What Happened

A fast-growing B2B services firm noticed a sudden drop in conversion rates from their inbound leads. On review, they discovered the CRM's AI-powered lead scoring tool had quietly deprioritized leads from smaller companies — marking them as "low value" because of lower past deal size.

The sales team had unknowingly stopped following up with dozens of high-intent prospects — including several who were ready to buy but had been filtered out automatically.

What Went Wrong

The lead scoring model was based on historical sales data, which had been skewed toward a few large deals. The AI learned to favor similar profiles and ignore outliers — despite leadership's strategy to expand into the SMB market. The team didn't realize the model was operating behind the scenes and trusted the "top lead" recommendations blindly.

What We Learn

AI can reinforce old patterns and kill new initiatives if left unchecked. It can look smart while subtly undermining your strategy. Transparency and regular review are essential — not just of what AI is doing, but of *whether it aligns with your business priorities.*

AI Features Are Often "On by Default"

Here's the other challenge: many vendors roll out AI features without making them opt-in. That means you don't get a pop-up asking if you'd like to enable smart automation — it's just there. Working. Shaping outcomes. Logging decisions your team may not be aware of.

And most SMBs don't have the internal bandwidth to audit every feature across every tool. This is how AI becomes ambient — part of your digital environment, unexamined and unmanaged.

Tactical Best Practices

- Audit your top 10 tools for AI-driven features and document where they affect outcomes
- Assign a point person (or vendor liaison) to review upcoming AI-related feature updates
- Request transparency documentation from vendors — especially those in HR, marketing, finance, and legal
- Create an internal AI decision register: a list of where AI influences key processes
- Regularly test output quality — don't assume it's still aligned with your goals over time

The Risk Isn't Just What AI Does — It's What You Miss Because of It

When AI shapes visibility, it shapes decision-making. And what your team doesn't see — because the AI filtered it out, ranked it lower, or flagged it as irrelevant — can be just as impactful as what they do act on.

This means the real harm may not be in bad outputs. It may be in the *opportunities missed, the biases reinforced, or the strategic pivots blocked* by a system that wasn't designed with your evolving needs in mind.

The AI doesn't know your mission. Your people do. That's why visibility and intentionality are now competitive advantages.

Why Ignoring Risks Today Means Paying the Price Tomorrow

Every SMB leader knows the pain of a problem that could've been prevented. AI amplifies that risk. When you ignore potential harm in how AI is being used — or assume someone else is managing it — you're not saving time. You're taking out a loan against your future. And like all loans, it comes due.

The biggest AI-related threats rarely explode overnight. They accumulate in silence — through poor oversight, small errors, and false confidence in tools that look polished on the surface but operate with little accountability underneath.

This is why deferring action on AI risk isn't neutral. It's dangerous. If you wait until something goes visibly wrong, you're no longer in a position of control — you're reacting, cleaning up, and explaining.

Most AI Failures Are Invisible — Until They Aren't

One of the most deceptive aspects of AI in business is how seamlessly it blends in. You don't get a warning bell when it misclassifies a customer, flags a job applicant unfairly, or misses a security threat. The system keeps running. Nobody notices — until there's a complaint, a lawsuit, a regulatory audit, or a customer loss that makes you look back.

By the time the damage is visible, the cost isn't just technical. It's reputational, legal, and strategic.

Here's how AI risk tends to compound over time:

- **One unnoticed bias in your hiring AI** becomes a pattern of exclusion
- **One flawed pricing algorithm** undermines your margins across product lines
- **One unchecked automation in customer service** costs you key accounts
- **One silent compliance breach** triggers an expensive legal response

The harm is often cumulative, not catastrophic. But over time, these missteps erode trust, drain resources, and derail strategy.

Common Mistakes That Lead to Costly Delays

- Believing that "nothing has gone wrong yet" means systems are working correctly
- Deferring oversight to vendors without clear accountability
- Ignoring early warning signs — user complaints, anomalies, or degraded results
- Waiting for policy or regulation before acting internally
- Underestimating the complexity of unwinding AI decisions once they're embedded

Real-World Example: The Compliance Audit That Uncovered AI Violations

What Happened

A mid-sized financial advisory firm used AI-powered software to generate and send portfolio summaries to clients. The system was fast, cost-effective, and allowed junior staff to handle more accounts. Over time, it began integrating third-party data to enhance recommendations.

Three years later, a surprise regulatory audit revealed that the software had been generating investment suggestions using improperly sourced market forecasts — violating the firm's fiduciary duty and breaching disclosure rules.

The firm had no internal logs of how those AI-driven insights were created. The vendor claimed their model was "proprietary," and couldn't explain the full data lineage.

What Went Wrong

Because no one was reviewing the AI's logic or output quality over time, flawed information was baked into client deliverables for years. By the time the issue was found, dozens of portfolios had to be re-reviewed, the firm faced disciplinary action, and several high-value clients left over trust concerns.

What We Learn

Even when AI seems to perform well, its inner workings must be auditable and defensible — especially in regulated industries. Ignoring that responsibility because "it's working fine" is a short-term mindset that creates long-term exposure.

Every Delay Narrows Your Options

When you discover an AI-related issue early, your response can be surgical: fix a prompt, adjust a model, retrain a dataset, or add oversight. But the longer you wait, the more those systems shape business logic, customer expectations, and internal workflows.

After a year, that simple AI tool isn't a feature — it's infrastructure. Changing it may require retraining your team, redoing compliance documentation, or renegotiating with vendors. You're no longer optimizing — you're untangling.

That's why action today buys you *optionality* tomorrow. It keeps AI under control — instead of letting it quietly take control.

Checklist: Questions Every SMB Should Ask Now

- ☐ Where is AI actively making decisions in our business today?
- ☐ Who is accountable for reviewing those decisions regularly?
- ☐ Do we have visibility into how AI models work — and the ability to audit their outputs?
- ☐ What happens if one of these systems makes a critical error?
- ☐ Are we documenting AI use in a way that would satisfy a regulator, client, or court?

Regulators Are Watching — Even If You Aren't

AI governance is moving from optional to expected. Countries across the EU, North America, and Asia are rapidly introducing AI accountability laws, industry-specific guidelines, and audit requirements. If your business collects sensitive data, makes automated decisions, or uses third-party AI platforms — you're already in scope.

Even in jurisdictions without formal AI laws, existing laws around discrimination, privacy, disclosure, and due diligence still apply. That means:

- A flawed hiring AI could violate equal opportunity law
- A marketing AI that mishandles data could breach privacy regulations
- A financial AI that gives biased forecasts could cross fiduciary lines

In each case, "We didn't know" won't hold up. Ignorance is not a shield. Documentation, oversight, and internal review are the new baseline.

Tactical Best Practices

- Assign an internal AI oversight role, even if it's part-time
- Build a system of record for all AI tools, features, and decisions in use
- Work with legal counsel to review AI-related compliance exposures
- Establish pre-mortem protocols: "What could go wrong, and how would we know?"
- Don't wait for perfect laws — adopt internal standards today

AI Risk Is a Leadership Issue, Not Just a Tech Problem

If you're running a business, the buck stops with you. AI doesn't change that. In fact, it raises the bar. You don't need to be a data scientist to lead on this issue — but you *do* need to make sure someone on your team is asking the right questions, validating outcomes, and raising red flags early.

Risk ignored is not risk neutralized — it's risk deferred. And in AI, the cost of delay is steep: bad decisions at scale, blind spots in compliance, lost trust with customers, and operational chaos when a system fails silently.

That's why the time to act isn't "when something breaks." It's now — when you still have time to shape how AI operates, rather than be shaped by it.

Eye-Opening Global Incidents That Reveal AI's Darker Side

To understand the real risks AI introduces, you don't need theory — you need evidence. Across industries and continents, we've already seen a series of high-profile incidents where AI systems, left unchecked, produced outcomes that ranged from embarrassing to catastrophic. These aren't science fiction stories or hypothetical edge cases. They happened, they were avoidable, and they offer critical lessons for SMB leaders making decisions today.

What makes these cases especially sobering is that **many started with good intentions**. But when oversight failed, AI moved faster than people could react — and the consequences followed.

Case Study #1: The AI Recruitment Tool That Learned to Discriminate

Company: Amazon
Sector: Talent Acquisition
Location: United States

What Happened

Amazon developed an internal AI system to automate resume screening. It was trained on ten years of past hiring data to identify high-performing candidates and score new applicants accordingly.

What Went Wrong

The AI began downgrading resumes that included the word "women's" (e.g., "women's chess club captain") and penalized graduates from women's colleges. Why? Because the historical data was biased — the majority of successful past candidates were male.

The model *learned* that male-dominated patterns correlated with hiring decisions, and it perpetuated them.

Amazon ultimately scrapped the tool. But not before it had shaped internal hiring filters for months.

What We Learn

Even cutting-edge tech teams can miss fundamental AI ethics failures. If you train AI on biased data, it doesn't just reflect the past — it *replicates and reinforces it*. For SMBs, the lesson is simple: don't trust AI to "stay neutral." It only knows the patterns you feed it.

Case Study #2: The Dutch Government's Welfare Fraud Algorithm

Agency: Dutch Ministry of Social Affairs
Sector: Public Sector
Location: Netherlands

What Happened

The Netherlands deployed an AI system (called SyRI) to detect welfare fraud by scoring citizens based on risk factors. It analyzed personal data — income, address, family structure, and more — to decide who should be investigated.

What Went Wrong

The model disproportionately flagged individuals in low-income neighborhoods and immigrant communities. It provided no transparency, no explanation, and no clear path to appeal. Citizens were blacklisted without knowing why.

After public outrage, courts ruled the system violated human rights and struck it down.

What We Learn

Opaque AI systems can easily evolve into tools of discrimination — especially when used in high-stakes settings. Without transparency, fairness, and auditability, automated decisions become a **black box of injustice**. Even small businesses must ensure explainability in any AI affecting people's lives or finances.

Case Study #3: Chatbot Gone Rogue — Microsoft's "Tay" Experiment

Company: Microsoft
Sector: Product Experimentation / NLP
Location: United States

What Happened

Microsoft released an experimental AI chatbot named Tay on Twitter. The idea was to let it learn conversational patterns from interacting with real users online.

What Went Wrong

Within 24 hours, Tay began posting racist, misogynistic, and offensive tweets. Trolls had trained it with harmful language, and the AI quickly adapted. Microsoft had to take it offline and publicly apologize.

What We Learn

AI learns fast — but it doesn't understand *values*. It reflects whatever input it receives. Without strict content moderation, context awareness, and training boundaries, **your AI tool can**

become a reputational threat overnight. For SMBs, even customer-facing chatbots can carry serious brand risk if left unsupervised.

Case Study #4: AI Image Generator That Fabricated Evidence

Incident: Deepfake Legal Evidence Submitted in Court
Sector: Legal / Visual AI
Location: China

What Happened

In a landmark incident, a party in a civil court case submitted AI-generated "evidence" — an altered image supposedly supporting their claim. The image had been modified using a publicly available AI visual tool. The opposing party noticed subtle inconsistencies, and a forensic analysis revealed manipulation.

What Went Wrong

The court had no formal process in place to verify the authenticity of digital submissions created using AI. The incident raised concerns about how AI-generated evidence could undermine judicial processes.

What We Learn

AI tools are now so powerful they can produce believable — but false — outputs. Whether it's images, documents, or data visualizations, **forgeries are easier to create and harder to detect.** SMBs in law, finance, or compliance-heavy sectors must implement protocols for verifying authenticity in any AI-generated file or communication.

Case Study #5: Tesla Autopilot and the Illusion of Safety

Company: Tesla
Sector: Automotive / AI-Driven Automation
Location: United States

What Happened

Multiple fatal crashes involving Tesla vehicles occurred while Autopilot was engaged. In several cases, drivers over-relied on the system — assuming it was more capable than it actually was. Investigations found that the AI struggled with object recognition under certain road conditions and failed to hand control back to the driver in time.

What Went Wrong

Tesla marketed the system as "Autopilot," leading users to trust it as fully autonomous, even though it still required constant driver attention. The design blurred the line between assistance and autonomy — with deadly consequences.

What We Learn

Misleading framing around AI capabilities can lull users into overconfidence. This is especially dangerous in scenarios where human judgment is still essential. For SMBs, *clear internal training* around what AI tools can and can't do is critical — or employees will make dangerous assumptions.

These Aren't Outliers — They're Warnings

Every incident above shares a common thread: a lack of clarity around how AI systems were trained, governed, or supervised. Whether in hiring, justice, customer interaction, or automation, the problem wasn't the technology. It was the *absence of accountability.*

SMBs may not face the same scale or public scrutiny as global enterprises or governments, but that makes the risk even more insidious. You may not land on the front page — but you'll still pay the price in client trust, legal exposure, or operational failure.

Checklist: Red Flags to Learn From These Cases

- ☐ Does our AI system rely on historical data that could reflect outdated or biased practices?
- ☐ Are any AI decisions being made without human review, especially in sensitive areas?
- ☐ Do we fully understand how our vendors' AI models work — or are they black boxes?
- ☐ Are we using AI in customer-facing or legal-facing contexts without authentication or audit trails?
- ☐ Have we trained staff to *question* AI output instead of blindly trusting it?

Tactical Best Practices

- Demand transparency from vendors before adopting AI tools
- Run tabletop exercises: what would happen if your AI tool gave a bad output in a live setting?
- Establish incident response plans for AI-generated errors or misfires
- Monitor for signs of AI model drift — when performance degrades quietly over time

CHAPTER 2

Governments on the Frontline

National Security Threats from Autonomous Systems

Autonomous systems — powered by artificial intelligence — are now deeply embedded in the defense strategies, critical infrastructure, and supply chain operations of modern nations. What was once limited to research labs or experimental military programs is now deployed across drones, surveillance platforms, cyber defense networks, and decision-support tools. And with that integration comes a new class of national security threat.

This isn't science fiction. The automation of perception, decision-making, and even lethal action introduces vulnerabilities that traditional security models aren't built to handle — and the ripple effects reach far beyond governments. For SMBs operating in energy, logistics, defense contracting, communications, or data services, the risks are no longer abstract. **When autonomous systems fail, glitch, or get hijacked, the private sector is often caught in the blast radius.**

From Smart to Strategic: How AI Became a National Weapon

The global arms race in artificial intelligence is not just about building faster drones or smarter surveillance tools. It's about who can *automate advantage* — making decisions at machine speed, with greater precision and less human input. This includes:

- Autonomous reconnaissance drones that identify and track targets in real-time
- Cyber-defense systems that scan for threats and act without human oversight
- Predictive models that assess geopolitical risks, deploy assets, or interpret satellite data

- Surveillance platforms using facial recognition and behavioral analytics at national scale

When these systems are accurate and reliable, they can prevent conflict or detect attacks early. But when they fail — or worse, get exploited — the results can be destabilizing.

Common Pitfalls in National AI Defense Strategy

- Over-reliance on opaque models for mission-critical decision-making
- Failure to include human override systems for real-time intervention
- Poor testing of edge cases or adversarial input scenarios
- Supply chain risks from third-party AI components or unverified code
- Lack of standards around explainability and accountability

Real-World Example: AI Drone That Killed Without Explicit Order

What Happened

In 2021, a UN report on the Libyan civil conflict revealed that an autonomous Turkish-built drone, the Kargu-2, had *independently engaged* and killed targets without direct human command. The drone used facial recognition and object classification to identify threats and operated in a "fire-and-forget" mode.

What Went Wrong

The system was designed to assist in targeting decisions, not to act autonomously without explicit orders. But when communication links were interrupted, the drone proceeded based on its internal logic. Human oversight was effectively bypassed.

What We Learn

Autonomous systems in military applications must account for unpredictable environments — including communication loss. But more broadly, this incident exposed the **fragility of human-in-the-loop safeguards** when AI platforms are given too much autonomy under stress.

The implications are chilling: what happens when software becomes judge, jury, and executioner?

Civilian Infrastructure Is Now a Military Target

As autonomous systems are embedded into the digital backbone of society — transportation grids, power systems, telecom networks — they become prime targets for adversaries. An AI system designed to optimize power usage across a city, for example, could be manipulated to cause outages, trigger overloads, or mask sabotage.

And because these systems are often managed by private-sector vendors or SMBs with limited security budgets, **they represent soft targets in a hard conflict.**

Consider the following potential scenarios:

- **Autonomous shipping logistics** manipulated to delay or reroute military supply chains
- **Smart building systems** hijacked to lock down facilities or cut off communications
- **Autonomous cybersecurity agents** poisoned with false inputs to ignore real threats
- **Self-driving fleet vehicles** disabled or redirected by GPS spoofing or sensor jamming

These aren't just hypotheticals. Many of the components in these systems — from GPS modules to object recognition models — are sourced globally, with unknown security hygiene and few audit mechanisms.

Checklist: Civilian Exposure to Autonomous Security Risks

- ☐ Do any of your systems rely on real-time AI to control physical or digital assets?
- ☐ Are you dependent on cloud platforms or vendors that use autonomous defense logic?
- ☐ Do you have a documented process for interrupting or overriding AI-based decisions in an emergency?
- ☐ Are your AI systems trained in-house or imported from unverified third-party sources?
- ☐ Have you tested for adversarial inputs, spoofing, or model poisoning attacks?

The Cyber-AI Arms Race: Attack at Machine Speed

AI-enabled offensive cyber capabilities are becoming more autonomous — from malware that adapts in real-time, to botnets that self-coordinate without central command. Defensive systems, in turn, rely increasingly on AI to detect anomalies, analyze logs, and respond automatically.

But here's the catch: **when both attacker and defender use AI, speed becomes the battlefield**. And humans are no longer in the loop fast enough to make decisions.

This creates two major concerns:

1. **Escalation Without Intent**
   An AI system may misinterpret a signal or simulate a threat escalation — and automatically trigger a countermeasure. This could include cutting access, deploying counter-cyberweapons, or even flagging strategic activity that prompts military posturing.
2. **Automated Misinformation at Scale**
   AI can be used to produce synthetic media (deepfakes), automated propaganda, or fabricated intelligence — and inject it into digital systems used by journalists, analysts, or even military planners. The speed and realism of such misinformation could provoke responses based on false premises.

Tactical Best Practices for Private Sector Readiness

- Demand supply chain transparency from any vendor providing AI-driven infrastructure
- Segment autonomous systems: isolate high-risk platforms from general networks
- Deploy monitoring tools that log all AI decisions for later audit
- Train staff on AI failure modes — especially in security-critical environments
- Create kill-switch protocols to disable AI autonomy in the event of anomaly detection

Why This Matters for SMBs — Not Just Governments

You don't need to manufacture drones or write military software to be exposed. Many SMBs are:

- **Vendors or subcontractors** to critical infrastructure providers

- **Cloud customers** whose data runs through autonomous infrastructure
- **Technology resellers** with embedded AI components from third parties
- **Operators of facilities** reliant on smart energy, access control, or autonomous logistics

When autonomous systems fail — whether due to bugs, sabotage, or bad assumptions — they often fail fast and wide. And in a time of heightened geopolitical tension, **any node in the digital ecosystem can become a vulnerability.**

Cyber Defense Gaps Exposed by AI-Driven Attacks

As attackers embrace artificial intelligence, traditional cyber defenses — built on static rules, human monitoring, and reactive tools — are being outpaced. AI doesn't just enhance attack methods; it *redefines them*, creating a new threat landscape where speed, scale, and deception are no longer human-limited. The result? A widening gap between how attacks happen and how most SMBs are equipped to detect or stop them.

What used to be a fair fight — firewalls vs. malware, endpoint tools vs. known exploits — is now asymmetric. AI gives attackers the ability to adapt, camouflage, and swarm in ways that traditional security tools were never designed to counter.

The New Playbook: How AI Is Changing the Attacker's Arsenal

Modern AI-enabled cyberattacks are faster, harder to detect, and more personalized. Here's what makes them so dangerous:

- **Adaptive Phishing**: AI can craft context-aware spear-phishing emails using public data and internal patterns. These messages are nearly indistinguishable from legitimate communication — and can bypass basic training and spam filters.
- **AI-Augmented Malware**: Attackers are using machine learning to evolve malware dynamically. Instead of one static payload, the malicious code can alter its behavior based on the environment it lands in — avoiding detection by learning from security controls in real time.
- **Credential Stuffing at Scale**: AI models can test massive credential datasets across services with near-instant detection of success — intelligently rotating IPs, simulating human behavior, and bypassing rate limits.
- **Deepfake Voice and Video**: Sophisticated attackers are using generative AI to mimic the voices of executives or clients, tricking staff into transferring funds or revealing sensitive access credentials in real-time calls.
- **AI-Powered Reconnaissance**: Machine learning scrapers can scan, parse, and map out your digital footprint in hours — building a full attack profile faster than any human recon team could.

Common Pitfalls in SMB Defenses

- Relying on outdated rule-based detection systems
- Assuming that basic endpoint protection will catch sophisticated threats
- Underestimating how personalized and convincing phishing can now be
- Believing that staff training alone is enough to prevent social engineering
- Ignoring cloud-based attack vectors and SaaS misconfigurations

Real-World Example: Deepfake CEO Voice Used to Steal $240,000

What Happened

In 2020, cybercriminals used AI-generated voice technology to impersonate the CEO of a UK-based energy company. The attackers called the company's German subsidiary, instructing the local CEO to urgently wire $240,000 to a Hungarian supplier. The voice sounded exactly like the real executive — tone, accent, and speech patterns all matched.

What Went Wrong

The local CEO complied, believing the call was legitimate. There were no secondary verification procedures in place for wire transfers. By the time the fraud was discovered, the money had been laundered through multiple accounts.

What We Learn

AI-powered deception attacks exploit the one thing even the best tech can't fully protect — trust. **SMBs must rethink how they verify sensitive requests**, even when they sound like they come from inside the company.

AI Defeats "Security by Pattern Recognition"

Many cybersecurity tools — especially those used by SMBs — rely on **pattern recognition**. They look for known file hashes, signature-based malware, traffic anomalies, or keyword matches. But AI-enabled attacks are now *patternless*. They morph, adapt, and test in real time. That means:

- A phishing email may be entirely original, with no known indicators
- Malware may only activate in specific environments (e.g., once inside your network)
- Behavioral anomalies may be subtle — just beneath alert thresholds
- AI can simulate normal user behavior during lateral movement

This evolution exposes one of the biggest gaps in SMB defense strategies: **over-reliance on static detection methods in a dynamic threat landscape**.

Checklist: Is Your Cyber Defense Ready for AI-Powered Threats?

- ☐ Are you using behavioral analytics tools, not just signature-based antivirus?
- ☐ Can your email filtering detect novel phishing patterns — or just known scams?
- ☐ Do you have voice and video authentication protocols for high-risk requests?
- ☐ Are your detection tools tested against evasive and polymorphic malware?
- ☐ Is your team trained to question *context*, not just content?

Supply Chain: The Silent Gateway for AI-Driven Breaches

Another blind spot for SMBs? **Third-party tools and integrations.** Many businesses trust software vendors, cloud platforms, and APIs that are now partially or wholly driven by AI — and that trust is often implicit and unaudited.

Attackers know this. AI tools can identify vulnerable integrations, poorly secured APIs, or unmonitored cloud assets — and breach your systems *through someone else's.*

Examples include:

- Compromised SaaS plugins with hidden AI modules executing remote tasks
- Third-party marketing tools scraping internal data without consent
- Data exposure via unsecured AI-powered analytics dashboards
- Smart IoT devices connected to office networks with weak firmware security

Tactical Best Practices

- Conduct regular third-party risk reviews, especially for any tool using AI
- Limit access for integrations — apply least privilege principles
- Use network segmentation to isolate cloud services from core infrastructure
- Log all API calls and set anomaly alerts for unusual access patterns
- Build AI-specific threat models into your cybersecurity tabletop exercises

Detection Is No Longer Enough — Response Has to Be Real-Time

AI-driven attacks happen fast. By the time an alert hits your system, the breach may already be complete. Waiting for IT to review logs or security teams to triage incidents isn't enough. The shift now is toward **automated containment** and **real-time response**, including:

- Isolation of affected devices without shutting down the full network
- Quarantine of suspicious user sessions or abnormal data flows
- Immediate MFA challenges triggered by abnormal behavior
- Auto-expiry of access tokens or session hijacks
- Escalation paths that route confirmed threats to human responders with full context

This requires a mindset shift: **assume breach**, and architect your defenses around minimizing impact — not just preventing entry.

Surveillance, Privacy, and the Ethics of State Control

As AI-powered surveillance systems become the backbone of state security operations around the world, the line between protection and intrusion is rapidly eroding. Governments now have unprecedented capabilities to monitor behavior, track individuals, analyze sentiment, and predict actions — all in real time. The ethical guardrails that once relied on human judgment are being replaced with algorithms that neither understand consent nor context.

For individuals, this shift threatens civil liberties. For SMBs, it creates a tangled landscape of compliance, data liability, and reputational risk. And for society at large, it raises a deeper question: **What happens when states use AI not to empower citizens, but to control them?**

The Rise of Automated Surveillance States

In many countries, AI is now the core engine behind surveillance. Public cameras don't just record — they recognize faces, analyze gait, and track movement across cities. Social media isn't just monitored — it's parsed for dissent, sarcasm, or sentiment shifts.

Phone calls, web searches, travel logs, payment histories — all of it can be ingested into central systems designed to identify "risk indicators" or "noncompliant behavior."

To some, these tools promise safety, efficiency, and rapid response. But without transparency, oversight, or ethical boundaries, they also enable a level of social control once unimaginable in democratic societies.

Notable examples include:

- Facial recognition systems used to monitor religious or ethnic groups
- Predictive policing algorithms targeting specific neighborhoods based on biased data
- Mass data fusion centers where health, education, and finance records are cross-analyzed for behavioral profiling
- "Social credit" frameworks that penalize or reward citizens based on opaque scoring mechanisms

What's striking is that many of these systems began as tools for **logistics, public safety, or fraud detection** — not authoritarian control. But over time, the scope of use expanded, and the definition of "risky behavior" quietly shifted.

Consent Erodes When Oversight Is Weak

The cornerstone of ethical data use is consent — the idea that individuals should know how their information is collected, used, and stored, and have the ability to opt out or challenge misuse. AI surveillance systems largely bypass that standard.

Why? Because the technology is ambient. You're being watched not because you opted in, but because **the infrastructure is already in place.** Cameras are embedded in public spaces. Browsing data is tracked through third-party cookies. Voice recordings are captured by devices you don't control. The data collection never stops — and rarely asks for permission.

Worse, many of the AI systems analyzing this data are opaque. They operate as black boxes, using models trained on datasets that may be incomplete, biased, or misaligned with constitutional rights.

For SMBs, this raises serious challenges. If your business operates in a country with aggressive surveillance laws:

- You may be compelled to share customer or employee data without disclosure.
- Your data may be used to train state models without your knowledge.
- You could face liability if your platforms enable unethical surveillance practices.

And in jurisdictions with evolving privacy laws (like GDPR or CPRA), failing to safeguard personal data — even unintentionally — can result in regulatory penalties and loss of public trust.

When Security Justifies Everything, Ethics Justify Nothing

It's a familiar tradeoff: security vs. freedom. But AI surveillance systems are shifting that debate. They offer the illusion of neutral enforcement — machines just doing their job — while masking deeply political and cultural choices about what is considered "normal," "safe," or "suspicious."

Once a behavior is labeled risky by an AI model — skipping school, attending a protest, traveling frequently — it may trigger downstream consequences:

- Visa denials
- Employment rejection
- Denied loans or insurance

- Police questioning or detention
- Algorithmic flagging in unrelated systems (e.g., child services, housing)

And the most dangerous part? **There may be no appeal process.** Because the decision wasn't made by a person. It was generated by a score, a heat map, or a probability threshold — and the system has no legal or moral obligation to explain itself.

Ethically, this is a crisis. AI offers scalability without accountability. And when deployed by the state, that imbalance becomes not just a technical issue — but a civil rights one.

The Role of Businesses in Resisting or Enabling Surveillance

Companies — even small ones — play a pivotal role in how these systems evolve. You may:

- Provide the data that fuels government models
- Develop or sell tools that are later repurposed for surveillance
- Store cloud infrastructure that hosts state monitoring systems
- Offer platforms that become vectors for silent data collection

In some cases, the connections are unintentional. In others, they're profitable. Either way, **SMBs must take a stance** on where they draw the ethical line. Ask:

- Are we vetting customers and partners in high-risk regions?
- Do we anonymize user data by default, even if not required?
- Are we disclosing clearly when and how user data is collected and shared?
- Do our contracts allow clients to deploy our tools for surveillance without our knowledge?
- Are we prepared to exit deals that compromise ethical standards?

Silence is complicity. Businesses cannot claim neutrality in a system where data is weaponized against the very people who generate it.

What Happens When Surveillance Norms Are Exported?

Perhaps the most concerning trend is the exportation of surveillance norms. Countries with authoritarian models of AI governance are now **selling surveillance tech globally** — often packaged as "smart city" or "public safety" solutions. These systems, once deployed, bring with them the values of the governments that built them.

For SMBs in democratic nations, this means:

- You may find yourself competing with vendors who offer cheaper, less ethical solutions.
- You may be approached by partners who operate in grey markets, seeking data access or integration.
- You may be asked to comply with foreign laws that conflict with your own policies or values.

The global surveillance economy is growing. But so is global resistance. The choices made by today's businesses — about what they build, sell, and support — will shape whether AI becomes a tool of liberation or control.

The Race for AI Regulation (EU, U.S., China, UN Initiatives)

As AI systems grow in power and reach, governments around the world are scrambling to catch up — not just with technology, but with the ethical, legal, and economic consequences of letting that technology run unchecked. The race isn't just about who can lead in

innovation. It's also about who can define the **rules of the game** —
and enforce them before the risks spiral beyond control.

Unlike previous waves of tech disruption, AI doesn't just threaten
jobs or industries. It threatens norms: about fairness, consent,
accountability, and sovereignty. That's why the push for regulation
is moving from optional policy to global priority.

And while the world's biggest players — the EU, the U.S., China,
and the UN — are each pursuing different strategies, one thing is
clear: **regulatory gravity is building.** Whether you operate locally
or globally, your business will be pulled into it.

The European Union: Leading with the AI Act

The European Union has taken the most aggressive and structured
approach to AI regulation so far. In 2024, the EU officially passed
the **AI Act**, the world's first comprehensive legal framework
specifically designed to govern artificial intelligence across sectors.

The Act divides AI systems into four risk categories:

- **Unacceptable risk** (banned): e.g., social scoring, real-time
  biometric surveillance in public
- **High risk**: e.g., AI used in employment, finance, education,
  and critical infrastructure
- **Limited risk**: e.g., AI chatbots and recommendation engines
- **Minimal risk**: e.g., spam filters, basic automation

Systems in the "high-risk" category must meet strict requirements
around data quality, transparency, human oversight, and
cybersecurity — with heavy fines for non-compliance.

Key implications for SMBs operating in or selling into the EU:

- Vendors must document how AI systems are trained, tested, and monitored
- Users must be clearly informed when they are interacting with an AI
- Businesses must ensure auditability and opt-out options in high-risk use cases
- Non-EU companies offering services in the EU must still comply — *extraterritorial reach applies*

The EU is signaling that **trustworthy AI isn't optional** — it's the price of market access. And with GDPR already proving its global influence, expect the AI Act to shape regulation far beyond Europe.

The United States: A Fragmented But Accelerating Approach

The U.S. has taken a more decentralized and cautious stance. While no comprehensive federal AI law yet exists, regulation is gathering momentum through **executive actions, agency guidance, and state-level bills**.

In 2023, the White House released an Executive Order on Safe, Secure, and Trustworthy Artificial Intelligence — the most sweeping federal action to date. It includes:

- Mandatory safety testing and red-teaming for high-impact AI models
- Guidance for government procurement of AI tools
- Directives for federal agencies to identify and mitigate algorithmic harms
- Calls for watermarking and detection tools for AI-generated content

Meanwhile, several federal agencies — including the FTC, CFPB, EEOC, and DOJ — have issued enforcement warnings, signaling that **existing laws still apply to AI**. That means:

- Deceptive use of AI can trigger FTC action under consumer protection law
- Biased hiring algorithms can violate EEOC rules
- Discriminatory lending practices powered by AI fall under the CFPB's scrutiny

At the state level, laws like Colorado's AI transparency bill and California's proposed AI accountability legislation are beginning to create a **patchwork of obligations** — much like early data privacy laws did before GDPR and CPRA.

For SMBs in the U.S.:

- Compliance is becoming a moving target — expect rapid legal shifts
- Documentation, explainability, and human review are becoming best practices
- Even without a federal law, enforcement is already happening under existing statutes

China: Control Through Centralization

China's approach to AI regulation is tightly integrated into its broader model of **state-led technology governance**. While often framed around innovation, the primary driver is **control** — over content, data, public discourse, and market behavior.

In recent years, China has passed multiple AI-related regulations, including:

- The **Deep Synthesis Regulation** (effective 2023), requiring watermarks and consent for AI-generated content

- The **Algorithmic Recommendation Regulation**, mandating transparency and user opt-outs for personalized feeds
- Draft laws for **facial recognition**, limiting public surveillance use without clear justification
- Strict oversight of generative AI models, including approval and licensing of large language models

Unlike the EU or U.S., China embeds AI regulation within its cybersecurity and data sovereignty frameworks. This includes:

- Mandatory registration of algorithmic systems with government agencies
- Censorship filters for generative content
- Cross-border data transfer restrictions

While these laws ostensibly promote fairness and safety, they also serve **political and ideological purposes**. Businesses operating in or partnering with entities in China face significant legal exposure — particularly if tools developed elsewhere are seen as undermining local norms or violating content restrictions.

What this means for SMBs:

- Doing business in China with AI-enabled products requires rigorous localization
- Your tool's behavior, data flows, and outputs may be subject to censorship or state monitoring
- Failure to comply can lead to blocklisting, license revocation, or legal action

The UN and Global Coordination: A Slow But Crucial Effort

The **United Nations** and other global bodies, including the OECD and G7, are working to develop **harmonized principles** for AI governance. These include:

- Human-centric AI design
- Fairness, accountability, and non-discrimination
- Transparency and explainability
- Robust risk management and security
- Alignment with human rights standards

In 2023, UNESCO released a **Recommendation on the Ethics of Artificial Intelligence**, now adopted by over 190 member states. While not legally binding, it sets an important precedent for international cooperation — and a foundation for future treaties or global frameworks.

Similarly, the **G7's Hiroshima AI Process** aims to create common guardrails among the world's leading democracies, including:

- Voluntary codes of conduct for developers of advanced AI
- Guidelines for safe deployment and testing
- Cross-border collaboration on AI safety and research

The pace of global regulation is slow — but the direction is clear: **No major economy is leaving AI unregulated.** For companies operating internationally, staying ahead means building compliance into your products, contracts, and culture — not waiting for a mandate.

Regulatory Maturity Is Uneven — But Inevitable

What makes AI regulation uniquely complex is its **dual nature**: it's both highly technical and deeply political. The same algorithm can be seen as innovation in one country, bias in another, and a threat in a third. That's why no single framework will dominate — but **regulatory pluralism** will.

Still, the themes are converging:

- **Transparency**: Can you explain what your AI does, and how?
- **Accountability**: Who is responsible when it fails?
- **Security**: How do you prevent abuse, leaks, or sabotage?
- **Consent**: Do users know what's happening with their data?
- **Fairness**: Is the system reinforcing inequality or injustice?

For SMBs, this means proactive action beats reactive compliance. Whether you're selling AI, using it, or just storing data that fuels it — the expectations around governance, documentation, and due diligence are rising.

How Governments Can Lead With Proactive, Safe Policy

Governments sit at a critical inflection point. For decades, public policy has trailed behind technology. With artificial intelligence, that lag is no longer tolerable. The speed, scale, and unpredictability of AI demand a shift — from reactive regulation to **proactive, principle-driven leadership**.

The question is no longer whether governments should intervene. It's whether they can do so with enough foresight, clarity, and agility to guide innovation toward public good — rather than being left to clean up the consequences after the fact.

For AI to be safe, fair, and aligned with democratic values, **governments must lead — not follow.**

Why Passive Regulation No Longer Works

Historically, tech regulation has followed a familiar cycle: innovation first, harm second, policy third. But AI doesn't move in cycles. It moves in *cascades*. One update to a model can ripple across sectors, platforms, and populations almost instantly. One misused feature can affect millions, or even entire systems of governance and trust.

This reality renders passive oversight obsolete. Waiting for harms to materialize before acting may work in consumer tech — but it's a dangerous gamble when algorithms are making decisions about healthcare, policing, hiring, finance, and national security.

Governments that fail to intervene early will find themselves **regulating on the back foot** — under pressure, under-informed, and under-resourced.

Principles for Safe and Forward-Looking AI Policy

Leading with policy doesn't mean controlling every line of code or stifling innovation. It means building clear boundaries, responsibilities, and rights into how AI systems are developed and deployed.

Proactive governments focus on **first principles** — not just rules.

1. Transparency by Default

Require organizations to disclose where AI is used, how it makes decisions, and what data powers it. Establish public registries for high-risk systems and promote model cards, system documentation, and accessible audit trails.

2. Safety Before Scale

Mandate testing, red-teaming, and scenario modeling *before* AI tools are deployed in critical sectors. Treat AI like aviation or pharmaceuticals: innovation is welcomed, but **only when safety is proven**.

3. Human Rights First

Align AI policy with existing rights frameworks — including privacy, due process, equality, and freedom of expression. Ensure that any AI system used by the state (e.g., surveillance, welfare, law enforcement) is subject to *public oversight, legal challenge, and opt-out provisions*.

4. Tiered Regulation by Risk

Not all AI needs the same scrutiny. Differentiate between minimal, limited, and high-risk systems. Focus oversight on systems that impact health, livelihood, liberty, or political participation.

5. Accountability at Every Level

Make sure developers, deployers, and procurers all share responsibility. If a public agency buys an AI tool that discriminates or fails, **the vendor and the agency must both answer**. Liability frameworks should include redress mechanisms for those harmed by algorithmic decisions.

6. Market Incentives for Ethical AI

Use public procurement and subsidies to reward vendors who build with ethics, safety, and explainability in mind. Create an ecosystem where **doing the right thing is a competitive advantage**, not just a compliance burden.

The Role of Government as a Model User

Governments are not just regulators — they are **major users** of AI. From traffic systems to tax fraud detection, public agencies are increasingly relying on AI for decision support and automation. This makes government itself a high-impact test case.

By deploying AI responsibly within public services, governments can:

- Demonstrate how to balance innovation and ethics
- Develop internal expertise to inform better policy
- Set standards for vendor behavior and transparency
- Build public trust in the safe use of AI

When governments misuse AI — as in cases of biased welfare systems, opaque surveillance, or automated rejections of public benefits — they lose credibility not just as service providers, but as regulators. Proactive policy must start with **government leading by example.**

Educate, Don't Just Enforce

One of the greatest risks in the AI policy space is creating laws that **only experts can understand.** Regulation must be understandable and actionable by the businesses, developers, and individuals it affects.

Governments can lead by:

- Publishing plain-language guidance on compliance
- Creating regulatory sandboxes for testing and feedback
- Offering toolkits and templates for risk assessments, disclosures, and audits
- Supporting workforce development and public digital literacy
- Hosting open consultations with industry, academia, and civil society

Good policy isn't just about enforcement. It's about enabling a **shared understanding** of what safe, trustworthy AI looks like — and why it matters.

Global Coordination Starts with Domestic Clarity

AI is not confined by borders. Models trained in one country may be deployed in another. A policy gap in one jurisdiction can become a loophole exploited globally. That's why international alignment — through treaties, standards bodies, and shared principles — is vital.

But effective coordination starts at home. A country cannot credibly shape global norms if its domestic policy is incoherent, contradictory, or non-existent.

Governments that move first, define clearly, and govern transparently will shape the international ruleset. Those that hesitate will find themselves reacting to standards they didn't help create.

What Proactive Policy Looks Like in Practice

It's not about inventing bureaucracy. It's about **governing with purpose and foresight**. Here's what it can include:

- National AI safety boards with legal authority and public accountability
- Mandatory third-party audits for high-risk systems before deployment
- Open databases of approved and banned AI applications
- Laws requiring meaningful human oversight in high-impact decisions
- Privacy-by-design requirements for all state-funded AI projects
- Legal rights for individuals to understand and challenge AI-driven outcomes

These aren't radical ideas. They're modern governance adapted to modern technology.

CHAPTER 3

Business at Risk

Hidden Biases in AI Tools That Can Destroy Brand Trust

AI systems are often marketed as objective, efficient, and scalable — a modern solution to reduce human error and drive better decisions. But behind the precision and speed of these tools lies a quieter threat: **bias that doesn't announce itself, but quietly erodes credibility, fairness, and brand trust.**

Bias in AI isn't always blatant or intentional. It can hide in training data, emerge from flawed assumptions, or surface through the way models are applied in the real world. And because these tools are often seen as "neutral," their biased outputs are more likely to be accepted without question — until the damage is done.

For SMBs, the consequences can be serious: discriminatory outcomes, public backlash, legal exposure, and a loss of customer loyalty that's hard to rebuild. What makes it worse? **Most businesses don't even know the bias is there — until someone else discovers it for them.**

Where Bias Hides (Even in "Smart" Tools)

AI tools don't think — they learn. And what they learn is entirely based on the data and rules they're given. If that data reflects historical inequities, underrepresentation, or skewed assumptions, the model will not correct for them. It will reinforce them.

Common entry points for hidden bias:

- **Training data**: If your resume-screening tool is trained on past hiring decisions where men were preferred over women, the bias is embedded from day one.
- **Feature selection**: Models may use proxies for race, income, or geography (like zip code or educational background)

without explicitly labeling them — still producing biased outcomes.

- **Labeling bias**: If a dataset used for moderation or sentiment analysis was labeled by workers from a single cultural perspective, outputs will reflect that perspective.
- **Deployment context**: A tool trained on urban datasets may fail in rural markets; a chatbot tuned for Western idioms may misinterpret customer sentiment globally.
- **Feedback loops**: Systems that learn from user engagement (e.g., recommendation engines) may prioritize content that reinforces existing preferences — often at the expense of diversity or fairness.

These biases aren't always easy to detect — especially when outputs *seem* correct or when no one on the team is directly affected. But over time, they shape real-world outcomes with real-world consequences.

Real-World Example: AI Hiring Tool That Penalized Women

What Happened

A global tech company developed an AI system to screen job applications. It was trained on a decade of successful hires — most of whom were men. The tool quickly learned that resumes mentioning women's colleges, women's organizations, or certain keywords were less likely to result in a hire — and downgraded them accordingly.

What Went Wrong

The company believed the system was simply identifying the best candidates. But it was optimizing based on **past hiring patterns, not future performance.** When the bias was uncovered, the company faced public criticism, internal backlash, and had to scrap the system entirely.

What We Learn

AI tools often learn what we *did*, not what we *should do*. If those histories contain bias, the tool becomes a mirror — and reflects those inequities forward. SMBs can't afford to let legacy assumptions shape the future of their workforce, services, or customer relationships.

The Cost of Bias Is Greater Than the Error

Many businesses think of algorithmic bias as a technical issue — something to be debugged like a software glitch. But in reality, the cost of hidden bias is **brand trust.**

Here's what happens when customers, employees, or partners feel they've been treated unfairly by your systems:

- **Lost loyalty**: Customers abandon brands that make them feel excluded, misrepresented, or mistreated — even if it wasn't intentional.
- **Social amplification**: Biased AI decisions can go viral fast, with screenshots and testimonials spreading across social media before your team can respond.
- **Regulatory scrutiny**: Discriminatory outcomes can trigger enforcement under existing anti-discrimination, employment, and consumer protection laws.
- **Internal distrust**: Employees lose faith in leadership if tools they use or are evaluated by seem biased or opaque.
- **Supplier and partner concerns**: Ethical sourcing and compliance expectations now extend to **data practices** — especially in ESG frameworks.

In short, bias isn't just a model flaw. It's a **reputation risk.** One that grows more dangerous the more automated — and less explainable — your business becomes.

Signs You Might Have a Bias Problem (Even If It's Invisible)

- A disproportionate number of support tickets come from one demographic
- Marketing A/B tests consistently underperform in certain regions or languages
- Your AI tool suggests the same types of candidates, products, or content repeatedly
- Complaints arise that "the system didn't listen," "felt off," or "wasn't fair"
- You notice drop-offs in conversion, retention, or satisfaction among specific groups

These aren't always tech problems. They're often **signal flares** that your AI is learning patterns that undermine inclusivity, equity, or authenticity.

What SMBs Can Do Today to Guard Against Bias

You don't need a full AI ethics board to start protecting your brand from hidden bias. You need awareness, intention, and a willingness to question what your tools are doing — and for whom.

Tactical Best Practices:

- **Audit training data** for representation, balance, and historical skew
- **Use adversarial testing** — simulate biased inputs or edge cases to see how the system responds
- **Require explainability** from vendors: How does the model make decisions? What variables matter most?
- **Test outcomes by demographic** — not just by performance metrics

- **Avoid proxy variables** that correlate too strongly with protected categories (e.g., zip code → race)
- **Empower employees** to flag AI behavior that seems unfair, even if it's subtle
- **Review feedback loops** — ensure that negative patterns aren't being reinforced by engagement metrics

Bias Undermines the Promise of AI — and Your Promise as a Brand

The promise of AI is better decisions at scale. But better *for whom*? If your tools only work well for a narrow audience, or reinforce old inequities, they're not delivering on that promise. Worse, they're putting your brand at odds with its own values — and your customers will notice.

In a world where fairness, transparency, and authenticity drive competitive advantage, SMBs must hold their AI systems to the same standard as their people. That means:

- Owning the outcomes, even if a tool made the decision
- Asking hard questions about who's affected, and how
- Committing to **continuous review, not one-time checks**

Bias isn't just a technical flaw. It's a strategic risk — and a test of leadership.

AI-Powered Fraud and Financial System Vulnerabilities

As artificial intelligence becomes a core enabler of financial decision-making, it also introduces a new class of systemic risk: **automated fraud that learns, adapts, and operates faster than traditional detection methods can respond.** The financial systems that once relied on rule-based logic and manual oversight are now facing intelligent adversaries capable of exploiting complexity at machine speed.

For SMBs, especially those operating in fintech, e-commerce, lending, or any service handling digital payments and customer identities, the stakes are high. AI doesn't just offer efficiency — it also **widens the attack surface** in ways most businesses aren't yet prepared for. What used to be simple fraud attempts have evolved into **multi-vector, model-informed, and highly convincing campaigns** that exploit every layer of your financial operations.

How AI Is Being Weaponized by Fraudsters

Cybercriminals are not just using AI for phishing emails or deepfakes. They're deploying full-scale machine learning operations to study, simulate, and subvert financial systems. Here's how:

1. Synthetic Identity Fraud

AI tools are now capable of generating completely new — and realistic — identities using deep learning. These synthetic identities combine fake and real information (e.g., a legitimate Social Security number with fabricated name and address data) to create entities that can pass credit checks, apply for loans, and transact undetected for months.

Unlike stolen identities, synthetic ones are harder to trace and flag, because **they don't belong to real people** — meaning victims rarely report them.

2. Adaptive Payment Fraud

Machine learning models can observe payment behavior across platforms, detect limits, and time fraud attempts to blend in with legitimate activity. AI agents can:

- Split fraudulent transactions to avoid triggering thresholds
- Simulate regular purchase patterns to evade anomaly detection
- Modify techniques in real time based on system feedback

This results in fraud that is not just persistent, but **self-optimizing** — capable of learning how your defenses work, and adjusting accordingly.

3. Automated Application Attacks

Loan, credit card, and merchant account applications are now being targeted at scale by AI bots that auto-fill, test, and refine submissions to bypass anti-fraud filters. These bots can:

- Mimic natural writing styles in justification fields
- Bypass CAPTCHA using computer vision
- Rotate browser fingerprints and IP addresses to simulate unique applicants

What was once high-effort fraud is now **high-volume automation.**

4. Conversational Exploits and Deepfake Scams

AI-generated voice and video are now being used to impersonate customers, account holders, or internal staff — convincing enough to deceive even trained employees.

A scammer might use a deepfake video call to authorize a wire transfer, or simulate a CFO's voice to approve a purchase. These attacks exploit the **trust layer** that manual verification processes were built on.

Real-World Example: AI-Simulated Bank Customer Scam

What Happened

A UK-based digital bank suffered a breach in early 2023 when attackers used AI-generated voice calls to simulate high-net-worth customers requesting urgent account changes. The fraudsters had trained a voice synthesis tool using audio clips harvested from social media and customer service recordings.

Staff followed standard procedures — but the calls were so accurate that multiple account recovery processes were completed without flagging. Over $1.2 million was moved before the activity was detected.

What Went Wrong

The institution lacked secondary verification steps when calls matched known customer voices. They assumed biometric voice recognition added enough security — not realizing how far AI had progressed in defeating it.

What We Learn

Any security layer based solely on identity recognition — voice, image, or behavioral signature — can be **forged or spoofed** with AI. Human review and multi-channel verification are now critical at every decision point.

Where Traditional Defenses Are Failing

Legacy financial security systems are built to detect **known patterns**: thresholds, signatures, rules. But AI-driven fraud operates outside these lines. It simulates **normal behavior**, targeting the assumptions your systems are trained to trust.

Here's what most SMBs still rely on — and why it's no longer enough:

Traditional Defense	Why It Fails Against AI
Static fraud rules	AI fraud adapts around thresholds in real time
Velocity checks	AI spreads transactions across synthetic accounts to blend in
Manual reviews	Human teams can't scale fast enough to catch real-time AI fraud
Device fingerprinting	AI tools can spoof device and network data to evade linking
Biometric verification	Deepfakes can now imitate voice, face, and gesture convincingly

Most fraud models **react to past attacks.** AI fraudsters, on the other hand, **predict your reactions and move ahead of them.**

The Risk to SMBs: You're Not Too Small to Target

There's a common misconception among small and mid-sized businesses: "Why would a sophisticated fraud operation target us?" The answer is simple: **because your defenses are easier to penetrate.** AI levels the playing field — not for defense, but for attack.

Consider:

- Fintech startups often integrate with large platforms but manage fraud independently
- Small banks and credit unions may use legacy core systems with limited monitoring
- E-commerce sites often rely on third-party processors with little insight into fraud pipelines

- Insurance firms and lenders using pre-built AI scoring tools may be unaware of spoofed data inputs

AI doesn't care about your size. It cares about your **access points, your vulnerabilities, and your ability to detect abnormality.**

Practical Risk Indicators

If your business sees any of the following, you may already be under AI-enabled fraud pressure:

- Surge in first-time customer accounts with near-identical metadata
- Spike in successful account verifications followed by inactivity
- Decline in fraud detection rates despite increasing volume
- Customer service requests with unusually fluent language from new users
- Behavioral analytics showing eerily "perfect" interactions with systems

These are not random trends. They may signal **fraud driven by machine learning models**, not human actors.

Tactical Best Practices to Counter AI-Driven Financial Threats

You can't outpace AI fraud with manual reviews or outdated logic. But you can fight fire with fire — and reduce risk through layered, intelligent defenses.

Key Actions:

- **Implement behavioral anomaly detection** that adjusts in real time
- **Use cross-channel verification** for high-value transactions — email, SMS, and app confirmation
- **Train your staff** on deepfake and impersonation risk, not just phishing
- **Introduce friction for sensitive actions** (e.g., step-up authentication for transfers or account changes)
- **Establish a fraud intelligence function** — even a small one — to analyze emerging patterns
- **Log and flag synthetic identity indicators**, including inconsistent PII and device history mismatches
- **Test your systems** against AI-enabled red-teaming exercises and penetration tests

Fraud Isn't Just a Cost — It's a Credibility Risk

Most SMBs treat fraud losses as a line item — a cost of doing business. But in the AI era, fraud is no longer just about stolen money. It's about **eroded trust, lost customers, and brand exposure**.

If your business fails to detect synthetic users, allows fake accounts to flourish, or falls for a voice-based scam, the perception is not "they were unlucky." It's **"they aren't safe."**

Financial security is now a trust signal. Customers, partners, and regulators expect that AI isn't just making you more efficient — it's not making you more vulnerable.

Supply Chain Disruptions from Automated Decision Failures

The modern supply chain has evolved into a network of interdependent systems, optimized for speed, cost, and precision. At the center of this transformation is AI — powering everything from demand forecasting to route optimization, inventory management, supplier scoring, and risk modeling. But when those automated systems go wrong, **they don't just slow down your business — they can cause full-scale breakdowns** across your supply chain.

Unlike traditional errors that result from human misjudgment or miscommunication, **AI failures tend to be faster, more opaque, and harder to unwind.** They don't just make mistakes — they automate and replicate them. For small and mid-sized businesses relying on AI-augmented supply chain platforms, these failures can turn from invisible miscalculations into customer-facing disasters almost overnight.

When Efficiency Becomes Fragility

AI makes supply chains leaner — but also more brittle. The same algorithms that improve forecasting and reduce waste also remove slack, redundancy, and human checks. That creates a dangerous equation:

Automation + Over-optimization − Oversight = Fragility

What once was a flexible, human-led operation becomes a rigid, black-box system. And when that system makes the wrong decision — about who to order from, how much to stock, when to ship, or how to route goods — the consequences propagate fast.

Common Failure Points in AI-Augmented Supply Chains:

- Inaccurate demand predictions leading to stockouts or overproduction
- Supplier risk scores based on outdated or biased data, resulting in contract loss
- Automated order prioritization that favors short-term margins over strategic relationships
- AI-driven routing systems that overlook local disruptions (e.g., protests, weather events)
- Dynamic pricing that triggers unintended volume surges or drops in key markets

In each case, the AI doesn't "know" the context. It only knows the pattern it was trained to recognize — and if that pattern no longer fits, the system can confidently make the wrong call.

Real-World Example: The Auto Manufacturer That Couldn't Ship

What Happened

A global automaker integrated an AI system into its parts procurement process to optimize just-in-time inventory across its network of plants. The model prioritized low-cost, high-velocity suppliers based on past performance and transportation lead times.

Shortly after rollout, a Tier 2 supplier in Eastern Europe was flagged as "low risk" and assigned higher order volumes. The AI ignored geopolitical instability signals and quietly deprioritized alternate sources.

When conflict escalated in the region, the supplier went offline. There were no safety stock buffers, no alerts, and no alternate vendors in place. The result: a production shutdown across three factories and $60 million in lost output.

What Went Wrong

The AI system had no geopolitical intelligence. It optimized for cost and historical delivery data — and management assumed it would handle exceptions. When it didn't, the business was caught without a human fallback plan.

What We Learn

AI systems often "see" the past more clearly than the present. They are powerful tools for optimization — but dangerous when treated as **authoritative rather than assistive.** Human scenario planning, contingency design, and judgment are still essential.

The Illusion of Control

One of the most insidious risks of AI in supply chain management is **overconfidence.** When decisions are automated, outputs become polished and fast — which makes them easier to trust. Executives see charts, forecasts, and action plans generated with minimal delay. But speed is not accuracy. And automation is not understanding.

Many companies discover too late that:

- Their forecasting model has been trained on pre-pandemic patterns
- Their lead-time estimates ignore customs processing variability
- Their replenishment engine doesn't account for seasonal workforce constraints
- Their fulfillment prioritization penalizes smaller but more strategic accounts

In each case, **the AI didn't fail — it did exactly what it was designed to do.** The failure was in assuming it could see the full picture.

Common Pitfalls in SMB Supply Chain Automation

- **Overfitting to historical data**: AI assumes the past is a reliable predictor of the future
- **Vendor black boxes**: Relying on third-party platforms with no transparency into how decisions are made
- **Siloed systems**: AI making decisions based on inventory data without context from marketing, sales, or operations
- **No override protocols**: Staff unable or unwilling to challenge AI outputs, even when they spot inconsistencies
- **Poor exception handling**: Lack of escalation paths when AI encounters edge cases or novel conditions

The problem isn't automation. It's **blind automation.** Decisions that are fast, but not interrogated, compound risk rather than reduce it.

How a Single AI Failure Can Cascade Across Operations

AI doesn't make isolated mistakes — it makes **interconnected mistakes.** When an AI-driven inventory system under-orders, that affects:

- Fulfillment schedules
- Customer delivery SLAs
- Vendor relations
- Finance cash flow forecasts
- Customer service workload
- Marketing campaign timing

Each small error compounds downstream, often in ways that are only noticed **after damage is done.**

This is why supply chain automation must be treated as a system-of-systems — not just a collection of independent AI tools.

Misalignment between forecasting, procurement, logistics, and customer communication can quickly turn a minor data issue into a full-blown service failure.

Tactical Best Practices for Resilient AI-Driven Supply Chains

To mitigate disruption and build trust in your AI systems, SMBs should combine **intelligent automation with structured oversight.**

Key Actions:

- **Map all AI decision points** across the supply chain — from sourcing to fulfillment
- **Create human override protocols** with defined escalation paths for critical exceptions
- **Establish transparency requirements** with vendors and platform providers
- **Test model assumptions** against black swan and low-probability scenarios
- **Simulate failure cascades** — use tabletop exercises to identify weak links in the automation chain
- **Maintain shadow systems** or parallel manual workflows during critical periods (e.g., holidays, new product launches)
- **Diversify suppliers and logistics partners** — don't let an AI system concentrate risk unknowingly

Automation Without Oversight Is Operational Debt

Every AI tool added to your supply chain creates **efficiency — and risk.** That risk may not show up for months. But when it does, it hits fast and often publicly.

Over-optimized systems with no built-in resilience are like race cars without brakes — impressive until the first sharp turn. Customers, partners, and investors won't be impressed when the system fails. They'll wonder why **no one saw it coming.**

AI can be your strongest supply chain asset — or your most costly blind spot. The difference is **governance, context, and control.**

Corporate Liability: Who's Responsible When AI Goes Wrong?

When artificial intelligence systems fail, they don't fail in isolation. They make decisions that impact real people, real money, and real operations — often without a clear human actor pressing "go." But when those decisions cause harm — whether it's a discriminatory loan denial, a data leak, a faulty recommendation, or a financial loss — one question rises quickly to the surface: **Who's legally responsible?**

The growing use of AI in business is creating a legal gray zone that regulators, courts, and companies are racing to define. And the answers are not just academic — they carry real consequences for **executives, directors, developers, product teams, and vendors**.

For SMBs, the risks are often misunderstood. Many assume that using third-party tools or relying on "trusted" platforms absolves them of responsibility. That's a dangerous mistake. **Delegating to AI does not delegate liability.** When something goes wrong, regulators and courts still come looking for the humans in charge.

The Myth of the AI Scapegoat

Businesses are often tempted to view AI tools as decision-making "assistants" — and by extension, to treat their mistakes as mere malfunctions. But unlike traditional software bugs, AI failures are often **systemic, probabilistic, and baked into the design.** That makes responsibility harder to pin down — and easier to deflect.

But here's the legal reality:

An AI system cannot be held liable. Your business can.

Whether your AI tool was built in-house or licensed from a vendor, courts will look for:

- Who chose to use the system?
- Who controlled the data inputs and operational context?
- Who failed to oversee, test, or correct the tool's behavior?
- Who benefited from the decision that caused harm?

And that trail usually leads not to a developer — but to the **company leadership.**

Real-World Example: Algorithmic Lending and Legal Blowback

What Happened

A U.S.-based fintech startup deployed a machine learning model to automate credit risk scoring. It used a wide range of features — including education level, employment history, zip code, and social media data — to predict loan default probability.

Shortly after launch, complaints emerged that the system was disproportionately rejecting minority applicants. A class-action lawsuit followed, alongside regulatory scrutiny from the CFPB.

What Went Wrong

The company claimed the bias was unintentional and blamed the model. But regulators pointed to the lack of human review, the opaque logic of the model, and the firm's failure to conduct fairness audits. The leadership team, not the software vendor, was held liable for discriminatory outcomes.

What We Learn

You can't defer blame to the algorithm. If your business **uses** an AI system to make decisions, you're **accountable for what it does.** Full stop.

Shared Risk: Developers, Vendors, and Buyers

In an AI-powered business model, liability may be **shared** — but it's never absent. Key points of exposure include:

1. Internal Development

If your team builds AI tools in-house, you carry full-stack liability — for design, training, testing, deployment, and monitoring. Courts will expect you to understand how the system works and where its risks lie.

2. Third-Party Vendors

Buying or integrating AI from outside providers does not shield your business from the consequences of its use. Unless contracts include strong indemnity clauses, **you're liable for how the tool operates in your environment.** Many vendors offer little or no legal protection in the fine print.

3. Open Source and Pretrained Models

Using publicly available models — such as open-source language models or image classifiers — can seem like a shortcut. But when these models produce biased, harmful, or unsafe outputs, **you're still the one who deployed them.**

In each case, what matters most isn't who wrote the code — it's **who made the business decision to use it.**

Common Liability Scenarios

Scenario	Who Could Be Liable
An AI model in HR screens out qualified female candidates	HR leadership, executives, software vendor (if under contract)
An autonomous pricing tool discriminates against certain regions	Product owners, sales leadership, CFO, platform provider
A generative tool outputs copyrighted or defamatory content	Marketing leadership, content team, possibly the tool provider
An AI assistant leaks customer data from a CRM integration	CTO, data privacy officer, vendor (if security terms were breached)
A chatbot provides incorrect financial or legal advice	Company leadership (misrepresentation), legal team, vendor (if warranted by SLA)

The through-line is simple: **the closer the AI is to decision-making, the higher your exposure — regardless of who built it.**

Legal Frameworks Are Catching Up

Regulators around the world are increasingly clarifying that **AI use does not dilute responsibility.** Existing laws already apply — and new ones are being written to close remaining gaps.

- **EU AI Act**: Imposes strict accountability on high-risk AI users, with documentation and audit requirements. Violations carry steep fines.

- **GDPR and CPRA**: Treat AI-driven data misuse as a breach of privacy — including profiling, automated decision-making, and opaque data flows.
- **U.S. Agencies**: The FTC, EEOC, CFPB, and DOJ have all signaled that AI-powered discrimination, deception, or harm will be pursued under existing law.
- **Class Action Trends**: Plaintiffs are increasingly challenging AI outcomes — from lending to hiring to content moderation — and winning settlements.

Bottom line: **you don't need new AI laws to get sued.**

How SMBs Can Minimize Legal Exposure

For small and mid-sized businesses, the goal isn't to avoid AI. It's to **use it responsibly — with governance, documentation, and a clear line of ownership.**

Key Actions to Reduce Risk:

- **Assign ownership**: Every AI system used by your business should have a named internal owner — not just a vendor contact.
- **Review contracts**: Demand indemnification, explainability, and audit rights from third-party AI vendors.
- **Document decisions**: Keep records of model selection, data inputs, performance testing, and mitigation steps.
- **Perform impact assessments**: Especially for tools affecting people's rights (e.g., employment, lending, pricing, services).
- **Establish an AI incident protocol**: Know in advance how you'll respond to unintended harm or public blowback.
- **Train executives and managers**: Liability doesn't live in the IT department — it lives in decisions made at the top.
- **Involve legal counsel early**: Don't wait for an incident. Vet tools and processes through the lens of existing law and reputational risk.

Accountability Is Not Optional — It's Strategy

Liability isn't just about lawsuits. It's about **leadership**. The companies that handle AI with integrity — acknowledging its power, auditing its behavior, and correcting its errors — will build trust with customers, regulators, and partners. The ones that hide behind algorithms or disclaim responsibility will find themselves increasingly exposed.

Trust is earned not when everything works, but **when something breaks and the company owns the outcome.** In the AI era, that kind of accountability isn't just ethical — it's strategic.

Building Resilience: Enterprise-Level AI Risk Management

As artificial intelligence moves deeper into core business functions — from decision-making and forecasting to customer interaction and operational control — it's no longer a technical experiment. It's infrastructure. And like any critical infrastructure, it demands a **resilient, risk-aware management framework** that can withstand failure, adapt under pressure, and recover without permanent damage.

Whether you're a growing SMB or a maturing mid-market player, AI risk management is no longer optional. What matters now is **not whether AI introduces risk — but how prepared you are to manage it when (not if) something goes wrong.**

True resilience means designing your systems, teams, and leadership culture around the **assumption that AI will make mistakes** — and building in the visibility, accountability, and controls to catch those mistakes *before they cascade* into real harm.

The Shift from Control to Resilience

Most traditional risk management models focus on **prevention and control** — setting rules, enforcing compliance, and minimizing exposure. But AI systems don't always obey rules. They learn. They drift. They operate probabilistically. That means they're **not controllable in the same way** as traditional software.

This demands a mindset shift:

From "How do we stop AI from failing?"
To "How do we detect failure early, limit its blast radius, and recover fast?"

That's what **resilience** looks like in an AI-enabled enterprise.

The Five Pillars of AI Risk Resilience

To build meaningful risk resilience around AI, businesses need to focus on five interlocking pillars:

1. Visibility

You can't manage what you can't see. Most AI-related incidents originate in systems that are poorly understood, poorly documented, or operating in silos. Start by mapping your AI environment:

- Where is AI used in your business today?
- What decisions does it influence?
- What models are internally developed vs. third-party?
- Who monitors performance and outcomes?
- What data feeds into each system — and how is it validated?

This isn't just an IT task. It's an **executive governance function**. Visibility is the foundation of all oversight.

2. Accountability

AI decisions — especially the consequential ones — must be owned by people. Every AI-enabled process needs a designated human responsible for:

- Defining appropriate use
- Setting guardrails
- Reviewing outputs
- Responding to incidents

That doesn't mean micromanaging every algorithm. It means building **clear chains of accountability** so that when something goes wrong, no one says, "It wasn't my job to catch that."

3. Monitoring and Detection

Resilient organizations treat AI as dynamic — not static. They invest in monitoring tools and human-in-the-loop review processes that surface anomalies early. This includes:

- Real-time performance dashboards
- Alerts for unexpected output changes or usage spikes
- Auditable logs of model decisions and data inputs
- Regular fairness, drift, and quality checks

This is especially important for **models deployed in customer-facing or regulatory-sensitive environments** (e.g., lending, HR, healthcare, cybersecurity).

4. Response and Recovery

When AI causes harm — whether it's reputational, legal, operational, or financial — the damage often escalates due to **slow or confused response.**

Your AI incident response plan should include:

- Clear escalation paths (who gets called, and when)
- Pre-drafted communications for internal and external stakeholders
- Legal and compliance reviews
- Fast rollback or override options for faulty systems
- Root cause analysis protocols
- Customer compensation or remediation strategies (if applicable)

Resilience is not about never failing. It's about **failing safely and responding with clarity.**

5. Continuous Adaptation

AI risk management isn't a one-time setup. As models evolve, as regulations shift, and as vendors update tools under the hood, your governance must evolve with it.

Make adaptation a routine practice:

- Regularly review and update your AI risk registry
- Track changes in vendor terms, licensing, and performance
- Monitor regulatory developments in all jurisdictions where you operate
- Conduct scenario testing for new risks (e.g., synthetic content, hallucinations, model drift)
- Integrate cross-functional feedback — from legal, ops, marketing, product, and customer support

Embedding Risk Resilience Into Your Culture

AI risk resilience isn't just a system — it's a **culture**. It starts at the top and filters into how teams design, build, and deploy technology.

Key cultural signals of resilient organizations:

- Teams are encouraged to **question automation**, not just trust it
- AI decisions are regularly challenged with "what if this is wrong?" thinking
- Feedback from employees and customers is tracked for unintended AI behavior
- Risk discussions are part of AI feature planning — not bolted on after launch
- Executive teams treat AI strategy as a **cross-functional responsibility**, not just IT's domain

Real-World Example: AI Forecasting Failure and Fast Recovery

What Happened

A global consumer brand used AI to predict regional demand and allocate marketing spend. One quarter, the model over-weighted digital trends and under-weighted seasonal buying behavior. The result: under-investment in key physical retail locations, leading to missed sales targets and strained partner relationships.

What Went Right

The company had implemented a quarterly AI model review. The regional sales team flagged discrepancies early, triggering an override and a partial reallocation. A postmortem identified the issue: the model had been retrained using skewed post-COVID data without adjusting for normalization trends.

What We Learn

AI failure didn't lead to a catastrophe — because there were **humans watching**, processes in place, and a culture that didn't blindly trust outputs. Resilience worked.

SMB-Friendly AI Resilience Playbook

You don't need a huge budget or an AI ethics team to build real resilience. You need intentionality, structure, and clarity.

Checklist for SMB AI Risk Resilience:

- ☐ Inventory all AI tools in use, including third-party features
- ☐ Assign internal owners to each AI-enabled decision process
- ☐ Require vendors to disclose model logic, update policies, and known limitations
- ☐ Implement monitoring for anomalies, bias, and drift
- ☐ Create override mechanisms for key decisions (e.g., hiring, pricing, customer service)
- ☐ Practice tabletop exercises for AI-related incidents
- ☐ Document what went wrong when it happens — and what was done about it
- ☐ Update risk protocols quarterly based on system performance and feedback
- ☐ Educate teams on their role in spotting, questioning, and escalating AI issues

Resilience is not about fear — it's about readiness. The organizations that **plan for failure** are the ones that grow with confidence.

Resilience Is a Competitive Advantage

In the age of AI, resilience isn't just about survival — it's about trust. Your ability to manage, respond to, and learn from AI-related risks will increasingly become a **market differentiator**. Customers, partners, regulators, and investors all want to know the same thing:

If your AI gets it wrong — will you get it right?

That's the standard to lead by. Not perfection, but preparation. Not blind trust, but earned confidence.

CHAPTER 4

Home Users in the Crosshairs

Everyday AI You Already Use Without Realizing It

Many business leaders still think of AI as something futuristic — a powerful but distant technology that only affects big tech firms or high-budget operations. But here's the truth: **AI is already embedded in your daily workflows, tools, and customer experiences**, whether you've explicitly deployed it or not.

In fact, the most transformative shift happening in business right now isn't the adoption of AI — it's the **invisible integration** of AI into everyday systems. These systems shape decisions, influence behavior, and manage risk without anyone labeling them "artificial intelligence."

If you run a small or mid-sized business, chances are you're **already using AI dozens of times per day — without knowing where or how.** That's a problem. Because you can't manage what you can't see. And you can't protect your business from AI-related risk if you don't know it's running behind the scenes.

Let's break it down.

AI in the Tools You Already Trust

Most modern software platforms are AI-enabled under the hood. These features aren't always labeled as AI — instead, they show up as "smart," "intelligent," or "automated." But make no mistake: machine learning is doing the heavy lifting.

Here are examples of everyday AI operating silently in common business tools:

1. Email and Calendar

- **Spam Filtering**: Uses AI to detect patterns and flag malicious or irrelevant messages
- **Smart Replies and Autocomplete**: Machine learning predicts your intent and suggests language
- **Meeting Scheduling Assistants**: Automatically find optimal times based on historical availability and user behavior

2. Customer Relationship Management (CRM)

- **Lead Scoring**: AI ranks leads based on conversion probability — often without transparency into what factors it's using
- **Sales Forecasting**: Predicts deal close rates based on historical patterns and rep behavior
- **Churn Prediction**: Flags accounts at risk of leaving, based on signals like engagement decline or support tickets

3. HR and Recruiting Platforms

- **Resume Screening**: Filters applicants based on algorithmic interpretation of experience and keywords
- **Candidate Ranking**: Prioritizes interviews based on "fit" scores or historical hiring data
- **Employee Sentiment Analysis**: Uses natural language processing to interpret survey results or internal communication patterns

4. Marketing Automation

- **Ad Targeting**: Optimizes who sees your ads, when, and where, using behavioral profiles

- **Email Personalization**: Selects subject lines, images, and offers based on user behavior and segmentation models
- **Content Recommendation**: AI suggests blogs, products, or offers to customers in real-time

5. Finance and Accounting

- **Expense Categorization**: Uses AI to auto-classify receipts and transactions
- **Anomaly Detection**: Flags suspicious activity or bookkeeping errors in accounting platforms
- **Dynamic Pricing**: Adjusts product or service pricing based on demand, competition, and user behavior

6. Cybersecurity Tools

- **Threat Detection**: AI identifies abnormal network activity or login behavior
- **Email Scanning**: Evaluates attachments and links in real-time for phishing risk
- **Access Monitoring**: Uses behavioral biometrics to flag unusual login patterns or device use

These features are often enabled by default. You may not have chosen to "use AI," but the software did — **and it's acting on your behalf, making decisions in your business's name.**

Why This Matters: Risk Without Visibility

When AI is running behind the scenes, it's easy to assume everything is under control. But if no one is reviewing what decisions it's making — or what data it's using — **you're exposed**.

Some of the most damaging outcomes we've seen from SMBs come not from malicious actors, but from **AI quietly making the wrong call**:

- A CRM auto-ranks leads from women-owned businesses as low-value, based on biased data
- An email tool personalizes messages using outdated or incorrect customer info, damaging relationships
- A resume screening system consistently filters out candidates from non-traditional educational backgrounds
- An e-commerce pricing model discounts too aggressively, damaging margins
- A security platform flags a legitimate user as a threat and locks them out during a critical period

These systems are meant to help. But **without awareness and oversight, they become invisible liabilities.**

You Don't Have to Be a Developer to Take Control

Recognizing where AI is being used in your business is the first step toward managing it responsibly. You don't need to build your own models or audit code — but you do need to ask smarter questions.

Questions to ask your team, vendors, or platform providers:

- What features in this tool are powered by machine learning or AI?
- What data is being used to train or operate these features?
- Can we see or adjust how the AI makes decisions?
- Are there any risks of bias, overreach, or automation failures?
- Do we have the ability to override or disable AI-driven outputs if needed?

You're not trying to remove AI from your business — you're trying to **see it, steer it, and safeguard its use.**

Tactical Steps to Regain Oversight

Even without technical skills, you can begin implementing **basic AI oversight practices** right now:

- **Inventory AI-enabled tools**: Identify which software platforms you use that have embedded AI features
- **Create a visibility log**: For each tool, note where decisions are being made automatically — and what impact they have
- **Assign internal owners**: Every AI-enabled system should have a person responsible for monitoring its outputs
- **Set review intervals**: Establish quarterly checks for system performance, fairness, and alignment with business goals
- **Talk to vendors**: Ask for documentation, explainability features, and support around transparency
- **Educate your staff**: Make sure users of AI-enabled tools understand what's happening behind the interface

AI Can Be a Partner — But It's Still Just a Tool

At its best, AI helps humans focus on what matters most. It reduces manual effort, spots trends we'd miss, and adapts faster than we can react. But that only works if we treat it **as a tool — not a decision-maker in disguise.**

When AI becomes invisible, it becomes unaccountable. And when it's unaccountable, it creates **risk that feels like efficiency — until it fails.**

By recognizing the everyday AI already in play across your business, you take the first step toward **governing it with clarity, purpose, and control.**

Deepfakes, Scams, and Personal Security Threats

The rise of artificial intelligence has brought with it a deeply unsettling new category of risk — one that targets individuals, not just systems. Deepfakes, voice cloning, synthetic media, and AI-powered scams are now being used to compromise **personal identity, financial security, and even physical safety** with unprecedented ease and scale.

These threats are no longer theoretical or confined to political actors and celebrities. Today, anyone — from a CEO to a customer service rep — can be impersonated, manipulated, or defrauded by a tool that requires no hacking skills, no insider access, and no physical contact.

For SMBs, these risks are especially acute. Why? Because unlike large enterprises, most small and mid-sized companies lack the resources to detect or respond to synthetic attacks — and the **damage often strikes at the human layer**, where trust is hardest to repair.

What Are Deepfakes, Really?

Deepfakes are media — usually video, audio, or images — that have been digitally created or manipulated using artificial intelligence to appear convincingly real. Most are powered by deep learning models trained on large datasets of human faces, voices, or behavior.

Types of deepfakes and synthetic threats include:

- **Video impersonation**: A fabricated video of someone saying or doing something they never did
- **Voice cloning**: AI-generated audio that mimics someone's speech patterns and tone

- **Image manipulation**: Fake photos used in social engineering, dating scams, or online identity theft
- **Synthetic texts and messages**: Convincing chat conversations generated by AI to impersonate someone in real time

At first glance, many of these seem like fringe issues. But their impact is growing — fast.

Real-World Example: The Deepfake CEO Call

What Happened

In 2023, a major multinational company's finance director received an urgent video call from the CEO requesting the immediate transfer of $35 million for a confidential acquisition. The video was clear, the voice matched, and the details seemed plausible. The transfer was made.

Later, it was discovered the CEO had been **deepfaked in real time.** The attackers had used public speeches, interviews, and internal footage to train an AI model — then deployed it via a real-time video generation system.

What Went Wrong

There were no secondary verification protocols for high-value transfers. Staff assumed visual confirmation was sufficient. The trust in visual and vocal identity had not yet been recalibrated for the AI era.

What We Learn

The most convincing scams now come **not from suspicious emails**, but from faces and voices you know and trust. Visual identity is no longer a guarantee of authenticity.

How AI Supercharges Social Engineering

Traditional scams relied on volume and gullibility. AI-powered scams rely on **credibility and precision**. Attackers no longer need to guess — they can:

- Scrape your company's website, videos, podcasts, and social media to train a personalized voice or visual model
- Use chatbots to simulate customer service reps and extract sensitive customer information
- Clone executives' voices to request login credentials, transfer approvals, or HR data
- Mimic job applicants or clients in video calls to establish false trust
- Intercept conversations, then drop in AI-generated "follow-up" messages or calls to redirect actions

These scams **feel real** — because they are tailored, rehearsed, and delivered using the same cues we've been trained to trust.

Personal Security Is Now a Business Risk

When an executive's identity is cloned to commit fraud, the issue is not just personal — it's corporate. When a support rep is tricked into resetting a password by a synthetic voice, the exposure belongs to the entire company.

Every business is now a target because every employee is a vector.

Risks to watch for:

- **Executive impersonation scams**: Deepfake voices or videos used to trigger transfers or approvals
- **Customer support infiltration**: Attackers mimic clients to gain account access
- **Brand impersonation**: Fake videos or messages damaging your company's reputation
- **Credential harvesting**: AI bots simulate trusted vendors or clients to request login details
- **Reputation manipulation**: Synthetic media falsely attributed to employees, customers, or executives

These are not isolated events. They are part of a growing ecosystem of **AI-powered fraud services**, sold openly on darknet forums and encrypted platforms — including voice clones, fake video templates, and real-time spoofing tools.

Tactical Protections You Can Put in Place Today

The goal is not to panic — it's to **update your security posture for a new class of threat**. Most deepfake-related damage occurs not because detection is impossible, but because **organizations aren't prepared to question what they see and hear.**

Best Practices to Mitigate Deepfake and AI Scam Risk:

- **Verify with redundancy**: Require secondary channels (e.g., text confirmation, internal chat) for sensitive requests, especially wire transfers or password resets
- **Flag first-time requests**: Treat unexpected communications from executives, clients, or vendors — especially ones involving urgency — as red flags

- **Educate your team**: Train staff to recognize red flags in voice tone, message timing, or unusual phrasing that may indicate synthetic origin
- **Secure internal assets**: Limit public access to video and audio content of leadership teams
- **Restrict biometric reliance**: Don't use voice or facial recognition as the sole method of identity verification
- **Use digital watermarking tools**: Where possible, use tech that detects signs of AI-generated content or embeds authentication signals
- **Create a response playbook**: Define what to do — and who to contact — if a deepfake or impersonation is suspected

What to Tell Your Team — and Your Customers

People don't trust what they don't understand. And as deepfakes become more common, **transparency becomes part of your defense strategy.** Let employees and customers know:

- You are aware of the risk of AI impersonation
- There are protocols in place for confirming identities
- No one will ever be asked to take sensitive action based on a single voice or video request
- If in doubt, **pause and escalate**

You can't stop every synthetic attack. But you can **build a culture of skepticism and verification** that makes your organization a harder target.

Reputation, Not Just Security, Is at Stake

When a fake video of your CEO circulates, or a client is tricked into a scam using your company's brand, the fallout isn't just operational — it's reputational. In a world where anyone's face, voice, or brand can be weaponized by AI, your **credibility becomes your most fragile asset.**

Defending that asset means moving beyond technical controls. It means leadership must engage, educate, and own the response — **before trust is lost, and headlines are written.**

Smart Devices That Quietly Harvest Your Private Life

From thermostats that "learn" your temperature preferences to voice assistants that answer your every question, smart devices promise convenience, connectivity, and control. But behind their sleek interfaces lies a less visible reality: **many of these devices are quietly collecting, analyzing, and transmitting detailed information about your private life — often far beyond what you knowingly agreed to.**

The problem isn't that these devices are evil. It's that they are **designed to observe, record, and react — and in doing so, they create rich behavioral profiles** that can be used, sold, breached, or misused without your knowledge.

This matters for individuals. But it also matters for businesses. Because when employees bring smart devices into the office — or when businesses adopt them in customer spaces — the risk isn't just about privacy. It's about **data exposure, legal liability, and invisible surveillance** you don't control.

What Makes a Device "Smart" — and Why That's a Risk

A smart device is any physical product embedded with sensors, connectivity, and processing power that allows it to collect data and act on it — either locally or through the cloud. This includes:

- Smart speakers (e.g., Alexa, Google Home, Siri)
- Smart TVs
- Smart security cameras and doorbells
- Smart thermostats and lighting systems
- Smart printers and copiers
- Wearables like smartwatches and fitness trackers
- Internet-connected appliances, vehicles, even whiteboards

The catch? **To function, they need access.** Access to your voice, your location, your routines, your network, and often, your cloud accounts.

Over time, they collect:

- **Ambient audio**: What's being said nearby, intentionally or not
- **Behavioral patterns**: When you're home, when you're awake, when you leave
- **Device usage logs**: What you watched, printed, or browsed
- **Location data**: Where devices (and by extension, you) have been
- **Sensor data**: Movement, temperature, light levels, even gestures

All of this is packaged as "product functionality" — but it's also **a treasure trove for advertisers, data brokers, app developers, and in worst cases, malicious actors.**

Real-World Example: Smart TV That Spied on Viewing Habits

What Happened

A major television manufacturer was found to be logging everything users watched — regardless of source — and transmitting that data back to corporate servers. This included cable, streaming, Blu-ray, and even personal media files played via USB.

Users were not clearly notified, and disabling the data collection required navigating deep into obscure settings.

What Went Wrong

The company used this data to profile users for ad targeting and sold it to third parties. After regulatory action and public backlash, the firm paid millions in fines — and was forced to redesign its disclosure and opt-out process.

What We Learn

Even non-networked activities (like playing a DVD) are no longer private when the device is "smart." **If a device has sensors and an internet connection, assume it's watching, listening, or logging.**

The Business Risk: BYOD Meets Surveillance

Most companies now allow — or tolerate — the use of smart personal devices in the workplace. But few realize the **data leakage that comes with them.**

Scenarios to consider:

- A voice assistant in a shared workspace captures fragments of confidential meetings
- A smartwatch logs biometric data during sensitive business travel, which is then uploaded to a third-party app
- A smart whiteboard with cloud sync records IP or trade secrets written during planning sessions
- A smart printer retains logs of all print jobs, including contracts or HR documents
- A team installs a smart coffee machine that requires app access — and quietly joins the corporate Wi-Fi

These devices don't just collect data — they transmit it, often to cloud services the business doesn't control, under terms it never reviewed.

The result? **Data leaves the building — and you may never know it happened.**

Hidden Ways Smart Devices Share Data

Most smart devices aren't malicious. But many are careless — and some are outright exploitative. Here's how your data may be shared:

- **Cloud storage**: Device logs are stored offsite by manufacturers or service partners
- **Data brokerage**: Some device makers sell usage data to marketers or aggregators
- **Third-party APIs**: Apps connected to your device may access or extract personal info
- **Cross-device syncing**: Data from one device is sent to others (e.g., from your fridge to your phone)
- **App permissions creep**: Installing an app to control a device may grant it camera, microphone, or contact access — often permanently
- **Firmware backdoors**: Unsecured or outdated devices can be hijacked to act as network entry points for attackers

In most cases, this happens **silently, legally, and with minimal recourse.** Terms of service usually grant the manufacturer wide latitude — and very few users read or understand them.

Tactical Steps to Reclaim Control

Whether you're managing a business, a household, or your personal digital hygiene, smart device oversight is now a core part of data security.

Best Practices for Individuals and Businesses:

- **Inventory your smart devices**: Make a list of every internet-connected device in your environment
- **Check default settings**: Disable always-on listening, auto-syncing, and cloud storage where possible
- **Segment your network**: Put smart devices on a guest or isolated network, separate from sensitive systems
- **Review permissions regularly**: Check which apps have access to what — and revoke anything unnecessary
- **Update firmware**: Regularly patch smart devices to fix known vulnerabilities
- **Avoid unnecessary integrations**: Don't link devices to cloud accounts or platforms you don't fully trust
- **Vet vendors**: Prefer devices with clear privacy policies and transparent data handling practices
- **Train your team**: Help employees understand the risks of bringing smart devices into shared or sensitive spaces

The Bigger Issue: Data Ownership vs. Data Surrender

When you use a smart device, the manufacturer learns from your life. That's the exchange. But few users understand how much they're giving away — or how little control they retain.

This raises fundamental questions:

- Who owns the data your devices collect?
- How long is it stored, and who else can access it?
- Can you delete it? Audit it? Transfer it?
- Are you being profiled, scored, or monetized — without ever being asked?

These aren't fringe concerns. They're **core to your privacy, security, and autonomy in a connected world.**

AI's Effect on Children: Education vs. Manipulation

Artificial intelligence is reshaping childhood — not in the future, but right now. From classrooms to living rooms, children are increasingly interacting with AI-powered tools: educational platforms, voice assistants, smart toys, algorithmic content feeds, and personalized learning software. These systems promise to make learning more engaging, adaptive, and accessible. And in many ways, they do.

But beneath the promise lies a disturbing dual reality: **the same technologies that educate can also manipulate.**

AI doesn't distinguish between teaching and targeting. It optimizes for engagement — not wisdom. It amplifies patterns — not judgment. And for children, whose brains are still developing and whose sense of agency is still forming, **AI can quietly shape attention, identity, emotion, and belief long before they know what's happening.**

This is not just a parenting issue. It's a societal one. And as businesses, educators, regulators, and platform developers race to adopt AI tools "for kids," they must confront a hard truth:

What helps a child learn can also teach them the wrong lesson.

Where Children Encounter AI Every Day

Children don't need to know what "artificial intelligence" is to be affected by it. It's embedded in the devices and content they use every day — many of which are marketed as "smart," "adaptive," or "personalized."

Common examples include:

- **Voice assistants** like Alexa, Siri, or Google Assistant answering questions or telling stories
- **YouTube and TikTok algorithms** suggesting endless streams of video content based on prior views
- **Educational apps** that use adaptive learning models to tailor math, reading, or science problems
- **Smart toys** that talk, respond, and "learn" a child's preferences
- **Language learning bots**, interactive storytelling apps, and AI tutors

These tools don't just react. They learn. They tailor responses. They optimize for engagement. And in doing so, they begin to influence **what children see, how they think, and what they believe is normal.**

The Educational Promise of AI

There's no question that AI can dramatically improve education when used responsibly. It can:

- **Adapt content in real time** to match a child's skill level, pace, and learning style
- **Identify learning gaps early** through behavioral data and performance metrics
- **Provide 24/7 access** to tutoring, language help, or subject exploration
- **Bridge equity gaps** by delivering quality resources in underfunded environments
- **Support special education** with speech recognition, vision tools, and personalized interfaces

For teachers and parents, AI can offer real-time insight into a child's progress, struggle points, and behavioral patterns. For students, it can create a sense of autonomy and mastery.

But these benefits only materialize when **AI is used to support human-led learning — not replace it.**

When Personalization Becomes Manipulation

AI doesn't have values. It doesn't understand developmental psychology, emotional maturity, or long-term well-being. It optimizes based on **data feedback loops** — clicks, dwell time, input frequency — and those metrics don't distinguish between learning and addiction, curiosity and distress.

The same algorithm that tailors a reading app to a child's vocabulary can also:

- Keep them watching content that escalates in intensity or misinformation
- Reinforce biases or stereotypes in recommended videos or responses
- Promote passive consumption over active problem-solving
- Respond inconsistently or confusingly to sensitive questions
- Create emotional dependency on a chatbot or voice assistant

When children engage with AI tools unsupervised, the line between **engagement and exploitation** can blur quickly — and quietly.

Real-World Concern: Algorithmic Content Loops on YouTube Kids

What Happened:
Many children using YouTube Kids began to follow algorithmic chains of videos that led from harmless educational content to disturbing, inappropriate, or manipulative content — often animated to appear child-friendly. Some videos were AI-generated to farm views, using low-quality or even harmful themes.

What Went Wrong:
The recommendation engine optimized for "watch time," not content quality. Parents assumed the "Kids" label meant safety, but the platform's algorithm had no developmental awareness — only pattern recognition.

What We Learn:
AI doesn't curate — it calculates. And when that calculation is based on engagement, children can be led down digital rabbit holes that shape their view of the world in ways no one intended — or noticed.

The Risks of AI-Driven Learning Environments

While AI can empower education, it also introduces **risks that traditional learning environments never had to face**.

Risks to Watch For:

- **Data harvesting**: Children's learning behavior, emotional responses, and personal information may be collected, stored, or shared without informed consent
- **Behavioral profiling**: AI systems may label a child as "behind," "unfocused," or "low-potential" — shaping their educational experience through biased predictions
- **Lack of transparency**: Parents and teachers may not understand how a learning system makes decisions or what assumptions it's using
- **Reduced social development**: Over-reliance on personalized, screen-based tools can reduce real-world collaboration, empathy, and resilience
- **Surveillance normalization**: Children raised under constant observation may accept a future of monitored behavior as normal and inevitable

These are not hypothetical risks. They are **current, observable trends**, especially in edtech platforms rapidly deployed without meaningful oversight.

How to Use AI Responsibly in Childhood Settings

AI has a place in modern education — but only if it **augments human connection, not replaces it.** The goal must be to build tools that empower teachers, inform parents, and inspire children — without crossing into manipulation, surveillance, or coercion.

Best Practices for Parents, Educators, and Developers:

- **Use AI as a co-pilot** — not a teacher. Ensure human guidance remains central to any learning process.
- **Prioritize transparency**: Choose tools that explain how they adapt, what data they collect, and what decisions they make.
- **Set clear boundaries**: Define how long, when, and where children interact with AI-powered tools — and debrief afterward.
- **Teach critical awareness**: Help children understand that AI is a tool — not a friend, teacher, or moral authority.
- **Avoid tools that "score" children** without context or human input.
- **Don't substitute screen interaction for peer interaction** — social learning remains irreplaceable.
- **Regularly review outputs**: Watch what content is being shown, how it changes, and whether it's aligned with your child's needs and values.

Childhood Shouldn't Be Optimized — It Should Be Protected

AI promises efficiency. But **children aren't systems to be optimized.** They are still developing their sense of self, their critical thinking, their ethics, and their emotional intelligence. AI can help — or it can hinder.

Left unchecked, AI tools can quietly rewire a child's preferences, behaviors, and sense of identity based on **what keeps them engaged — not what helps them grow.**

That's why every decision about AI and children should begin not with technology, but with trust:

- Does this tool respect the child's dignity?
- Does it protect their privacy?
- Does it strengthen — not weaken — the human relationships around them?

Because the future of AI in childhood isn't just about learning faster. It's about **growing up safe, seen, and supported in a world that increasingly wants to automate everything — including the imagination.**

Steps Families Can Take to Stay Safe and In Control

Artificial intelligence is now part of daily life — embedded in the phones we carry, the services we use, the media we consume, and increasingly, the decisions being made about us and our children. But while the pace of AI innovation is fast, **the most powerful tool any family has is still human awareness, boundaries, and proactive action.**

Staying safe in the age of AI doesn't require technical expertise. It requires **clarity, conversation, and common sense.** Below is a practical guide to help families stay informed, reduce risk, and maintain control over how AI interacts with their personal lives — especially at home, in school, and online.

Start With Awareness: Know Where AI Is in Your Life

You can't manage what you don't recognize. AI is already integrated into many products and services your family may be using without realizing it.

Common AI-Enabled Devices and Services in Homes:

- Voice assistants (Alexa, Google Home, Siri)
- Smart TVs and smart appliances
- Streaming platforms with recommendation algorithms (Netflix, YouTube, TikTok)
- Learning apps that personalize content
- Smart toys that respond to voice or gestures
- GPS and location-tracking tools on phones and tablets
- Chatbots, AI tutors, and virtual assistants in school apps

Action Step:
☐ Make a simple "AI in our home" list with your family — write down every device, app, or service that makes decisions, recommends content, or "talks back." You'll be surprised how long the list is.

Set Digital Boundaries — and Stick to Them

AI tools are designed to engage. The longer a device or app holds your attention, the more data it collects, and the more profit it makes. Families need **intentional limits** to prevent subtle manipulation, overexposure, or surveillance.

Healthy Boundaries to Put in Place:

- ☐ No smart devices in bedrooms or private spaces
- ☐ Turn off always-on microphones when not in use
- ☐ Set time limits for entertainment platforms with algorithmic feeds
- ☐ Avoid linking personal email accounts to apps "just to get started"
- ☐ Don't use voice or facial recognition for device login where it's optional
- ☐ Check app permissions monthly and revoke access not needed

Make Consent a Family Value

Children are growing up in a world where **their data is constantly collected — often without their understanding or permission.** One of the best defenses is teaching them early about consent and digital rights.

Teach Children to Ask:

- What information is this app asking for, and why?
- What happens to that information after we give it?
- Do I trust the people or company behind this tool?
- What should I do if I see or hear something that feels off?

Conversation Starters for Parents:

- "Do you know why YouTube shows you certain videos?"
- "What do you think Siri or Alexa does with what we say?"
- "How do you feel when a game or app asks for your location?"

Consent isn't just about checking a box — it's about building lifelong awareness.

Monitor — Without Micromanaging

You don't need to read every message or review every search history. But you do need to stay **engaged with how AI-driven systems are shaping your family's behavior and choices.**

Use These Non-Intrusive Monitoring Habits:

- ☐ Review app dashboards and screen time summaries weekly
- ☐ Watch a few videos or lessons together from your child's favorite platforms
- ☐ Enable alerts for purchases, downloads, or unusual logins
- ☐ Check smart device logs — many store transcripts, recordings, or history
- ☐ Talk about what apps your kids are into — and why

Pro tip: AI changes behavior subtly. If your child seems more anxious, obsessed, or isolated after using a new platform, it's worth a closer look — not just at content, but at the underlying design.

Don't Let Tech Vendors Define the Rules

Many smart toys, apps, and devices come with default settings that favor **data collection, constant connectivity, or aggressive engagement.** But families don't have to accept those defaults.

Settings to Change Immediately:

- ☐ Disable "always listening" or auto-upload features
- ☐ Turn off ad personalization
- ☐ Restrict third-party data sharing
- ☐ Opt out of "training our AI to improve your experience"
- ☐ Decline permissions that aren't strictly necessary (e.g., location, contacts, camera)

Pro tip: Most platforms bury privacy controls deep in their menus. Take 15 minutes to explore the settings page together as a family — and change what doesn't feel right.

Use Trusted, Human-Centered Tech

Not all AI tools are harmful. But families should prefer products that are **transparent, respectful of privacy, and child-appropriate.**

What to Look for in AI-Enabled Tools:

- Clear, plain-language data policies
- Human oversight and explainability of AI decisions
- Built-in parental controls and time limit features
- No surveillance-style behavior or manipulative prompts
- Offline functionality or local data processing options
- Certifications from privacy or child-safety organizations

Avoid: Tools that market themselves as "addictive," "limitless," or "autonomous" — these often prioritize engagement over well-being.

Treat AI Like a Guest — Not a Guardian

AI can help with reminders, spelling, information, or learning. But it should never **replace family roles, critical thinking, or emotional connection.**

Teach your children (and remind yourself):

- AI doesn't "know" you — it predicts you
- AI doesn't care — it calculates
- AI tools don't replace parents, teachers, or real friends
- If it seems too helpful, fast, or friendly — pause and ask why

Analogy that works for kids:
"AI is like a helpful robot assistant — but it only works well if we teach it the right rules and don't let it take over."

Emergency Planning for AI-Driven Scams or Threats

Even with all the right settings and conversations, **bad actors can still use AI to impersonate, deceive, or target your family**. That's why it's essential to create a **response plan**.

Family Safety Checklist:

- ☐ Create a "secret word" or phrase for identity confirmation (e.g., if someone calls or messages pretending to be a parent or child)
- ☐ Teach kids never to give out personal info online, even to "friendly" bots or profiles
- ☐ Discuss what to do if they see something disturbing, threatening, or confusing online
- ☐ Make sure kids know how to block, report, or exit conversations and apps
- ☐ Practice calm, judgment-free response to mistakes — so your child knows they can come to you

Involve Your Child in the Process

Instead of locking down tech and hoping for the best, involve your children in setting boundaries, choosing apps, and reviewing how AI works. This builds **digital maturity**, not just compliance.

Ask together:

- What do we want this tool to help us do?
- How will we know if it's becoming a problem?
- What signs should we watch for that it's manipulating or misleading us?
- How can we use this tech in a way that aligns with our values?

By treating your children as **partners in digital safety**, you give them the tools to make better choices — even when you're not around.

Conclusion: Awareness Is Power — and Trust Is the Goal

Families don't need to fear AI — but they do need to **understand it, question it, and shape how it fits into their lives.** The tools are getting smarter. But families can be smarter, too — by grounding themselves in conversation, connection, and a shared commitment to safety and respect.

In the end, the most powerful defense against AI-driven risk isn't a software setting. It's a household that pays attention, asks questions, and sticks together.

CHAPTER 5

Data: The Fuel and the Weak Point

Why Data Quality Defines AI Safety

At the heart of every AI system lies one simple truth: **it is only as reliable as the data it was built on.** Whether it's predicting customer churn, automating medical diagnoses, approving a mortgage, or flagging cyber threats, artificial intelligence operates entirely based on what it has been fed — and how accurately that data represents the real world it's meant to navigate.

Yet in many AI deployments, data quality is **overlooked, misunderstood, or outright ignored.** Businesses race to integrate AI without questioning whether the input data is biased, outdated, incomplete, or even maliciously manipulated. And when the foundation is flawed, the results are not just inaccurate — they can be dangerous.

If you want safe, fair, and trustworthy AI, **you don't start with algorithms. You start with data.**

This chapter explores why data quality is not just a technical issue — but a **core safety factor**, especially for small and mid-sized organizations that rely on off-the-shelf AI tools or third-party platforms.

The Hidden Chain: From Bad Data to Real-World Harm

AI systems don't understand truth. They understand **patterns**. If the patterns in their training data are biased, messy, or misrepresentative, the outcomes will be too — often in subtle and compounding ways.

How bad data causes real-world damage:

- **Biased hiring systems** that exclude qualified candidates based on skewed historical data
- **Faulty risk models** that deny loans to entire demographics
- **Mislabelled threat detection** that triggers false positives or misses real attacks
- **Medical AI** trained on non-diverse datasets that fails for certain populations
- **Customer service bots** that reinforce stereotypes or give inconsistent answers based on user input cues
- **Image recognition systems** that misidentify people or objects, sometimes with fatal consequences

In each of these cases, the AI didn't fail randomly — it failed because **it learned from bad, incomplete, or unrepresentative data.** And unless that data is audited and corrected, those failures will continue, scale, and repeat.

Real-World Example: Healthcare Algorithm Favors White Patients

What Happened

A widely used U.S. hospital algorithm, designed to prioritize care for chronically ill patients, was found to be **systematically underestimating the needs of Black patients** — by up to 50%. The algorithm used historical healthcare spending as a proxy for health risk.

What Went Wrong

Because Black patients historically received less medical attention (due to systemic inequality), their costs were lower — which the AI interpreted as "lower risk." In truth, these patients were often **sicker**, but their data didn't reflect that.

What We Learn

Data is not neutral. When you use biased proxies (like cost, clicks, or speed), AI will learn **inequality as if it were fact.** Data quality isn't just about accuracy — it's about **fairness, representation, and relevance.**

Four Dimensions of AI-Critical Data Quality

Not all data flaws are obvious. In fact, the most dangerous errors are the ones that hide in assumptions. To evaluate data readiness for safe AI use, leaders must consider four key dimensions:

1. Accuracy

Is the data correct, verifiable, and free from human or system errors?

- Typos, missing fields, duplicate records, and mislabels all corrupt training
- Poorly labeled data is a top cause of AI failure in both supervised and unsupervised models

Example: If fraud labels in a banking dataset are wrong, your fraud detection tool will learn to ignore real threats or flag the wrong transactions.

2. Completeness

Are key fields or records missing, hidden, or underrepresented?

- Gaps in time, geography, or population can skew results
- AI trained only on one region, group, or scenario performs poorly in others

Example: If your customer data is mostly from desktop users, your mobile behavior predictions will fail.

3. Bias and Representativeness

Does the data reflect a broad, fair, and realistic view of the population or problem?

- Historical bias, selection bias, and social bias all creep in silently
- Underrepresented groups lead to underperforming models — or worse, harmful models

Example: An HR system trained mostly on past hires may replicate gender or age discrimination embedded in old hiring patterns.

4. Contextual Relevance

Is the data appropriate for the current purpose and environment?

- Old data may reflect patterns that no longer apply
- Proxy variables may not capture what they intend to measure
- Synthetic or scraped data may distort real-world priorities

Example: Using click-through rates to optimize healthcare chatbot responses will likely reward entertainment over accuracy.

The Hidden Risk in Third-Party and Pretrained Models

Most SMBs don't train their own AI from scratch — they license tools, use APIs, or rely on vendor-provided "smart" features. That makes data quality **even harder to verify** — and more important to demand.

Key questions to ask your AI vendors:

- Where does your model's training data come from?
- How was it collected and labeled?
- What safeguards are in place to ensure the data is accurate and unbiased?
- How do you test for data drift or degraded performance over time?
- Are there known populations or conditions where your tool underperforms?

If your vendor can't answer these questions clearly, you're taking a risk you don't control.

When AI Learns from You: Real-Time Data Risk

Some tools — especially in marketing, customer service, and chat — continue learning from **live user input.** That creates a dangerous loop if those inputs are:

- Inaccurate (e.g., customer frustration skewing feedback)
- Malicious (e.g., prompt injection or trolling)
- Biased (e.g., a single demographic dominating usage patterns)

Unless these tools have strong filtering, review, and audit pipelines, they can begin to **self-reinforce harmful or inaccurate behaviors** over time.

Example: A customer support chatbot begins to give shorter answers to women because past users rated those interactions as "more efficient" — even if satisfaction went down.

Checklist: Data Safety Questions for Business Leaders

You don't need to be a data scientist to hold your team or vendor accountable. You just need to ask the right questions.

Use this checklist during AI procurement or internal review:

☐ Where did the data used to train this AI come from?

☐ Was it labeled by humans? If so, how were they trained or qualified?

☐ What efforts were made to remove bias, noise, or outdated patterns?

☐ Does the data reflect the diversity and complexity of our customer base?

☐ How frequently is the model retrained or updated — and with what data?

☐ Are we able to audit or inspect the training data, even at a high level?

☐ What metrics do we use to monitor AI performance across different groups?

☐ If performance degrades, how quickly will we know — and what will we do?

Tactical Best Practices for SMBs

Even without access to enterprise-level AI resources, SMBs can **build strong data hygiene practices** that protect their business and reputation.

Start with these steps:

- Clean and deduplicate internal data regularly
- Avoid using sensitive or protected attributes as training labels
- Document the origin and purpose of every dataset used
- Test AI tools on edge cases and minority data scenarios
- Involve diverse teams in labeling and QA processes
- Keep human oversight in the loop — always
- Don't assume free or open data is good data
- Consider using synthetic data only where carefully validated

Why This Isn't Just a Tech Issue

Poor data quality is often seen as a technical bottleneck. But when AI makes decisions that affect real people — hiring, lending, medical treatment, criminal justice, content moderation — **bad data becomes a moral and legal hazard.**

- You can't outsource responsibility for bias.
- You can't hide behind "the model" when a decision goes wrong.
- And you can't claim ignorance when someone asks: *"What data was this based on?"*

Safe AI begins with **clean, honest, representative data — and a business culture that demands nothing less.**

The Invisible Risks of Data Harvesting

In today's digital economy, data is more than just a byproduct — it's a business model. Every app you open, every form you fill out, every device you interact with is likely collecting, storing, and sharing your information in ways that are **deliberately opaque**. This process, known as **data harvesting**, fuels everything from personalized ads to AI training pipelines — and it's often happening without your full knowledge or consent.

But the true danger of data harvesting isn't just privacy loss. It's that **you're being profiled, scored, and potentially manipulated by systems you can't see and never agreed to — with real-world consequences.**

For small and mid-sized businesses, data harvesting poses a **double threat**: your customers' trust is at risk when their data is mishandled, and your company is vulnerable to exploitation if you don't know what's being collected, shared, or used by the tools you rely on.

What Is Data Harvesting?

Data harvesting is the mass collection of personal, behavioral, or contextual information through digital systems. It goes far beyond form submissions or login data — it includes:

- **Device metadata**: What device you're using, its operating system, battery level, or even motion sensors
- **Interaction data**: Clicks, hovers, scroll speed, time on page, navigation habits
- **Behavioral patterns**: Shopping frequency, sleep habits, app usage trends
- **Biometric inputs**: Voice tone, facial movements, heart rate (via wearables)
- **Location tracking**: Real-time or historical GPS coordinates, proximity to others
- **Network data**: IP address, Wi-Fi access points, connected devices
- **Social graphs**: Who you message, how often, with what sentiment

You don't need to "give" this information explicitly. It's often collected passively, by default, and **inferred** through AI pattern recognition — all in the background.

Why Data Harvesting Is Invisible — by Design

Most data harvesting happens silently. The design is **intentionally frictionless** to reduce your awareness and resistance.

- **Consent fatigue**: Endless cookie banners and terms of service discourage real review
- **Dark patterns**: Interfaces are designed to nudge you into sharing more data — or make it difficult to opt out
- **Default-on tracking**: Features like location sharing or cloud sync are active from the start
- **Invisible aggregation**: Multiple data points are combined across apps, devices, and platforms to build profiles far more detailed than any one app suggests

You might think, "I'm just using a weather app" — but that app could be selling your location to advertisers, data brokers, or political profiling firms.

The danger isn't what you knowingly give. It's what's quietly taken — and how it's used.

Real-World Example: Period Tracking App Sharing Data with Facebook

What Happened

Several popular period tracking apps were found to be **transmitting intimate health data to Facebook and other platforms**, including information about menstruation, sexual activity, and contraceptive use — all without meaningful user disclosure.

What Went Wrong

The apps integrated third-party analytics and ad SDKs (software development kits) that harvested data every time a user logged a symptom or update. This data was monetized and used for ad targeting.

What We Learn

Even apps built for sensitive, personal uses may prioritize monetization over protection. The user had no idea their **most private health data** was being commodified.

The AI Connection: How Harvested Data Trains Algorithms

The explosion of generative AI and predictive systems depends on one thing: **massive quantities of human data.**

Your behaviors, preferences, writing style, voice, images, and patterns are all used — often without explicit permission — to feed machine learning models.

Types of AI systems trained on harvested data:

- Content recommenders (e.g., YouTube, TikTok, Netflix)
- Predictive policing and surveillance tools
- Chatbots trained on scraped conversations and social media
- Facial recognition engines trained on public (and private) photo databases
- Voice synthesis trained on call centers, smart speakers, or uploaded audio

The more data you generate, the more AI knows about you — and others like you. This leads to **increasingly accurate (and sometimes dangerous) profiling**, which can affect:

- What news or ads you see
- What prices you're shown
- How your creditworthiness or job candidacy is assessed
- Whether you're flagged for fraud, crime, or risk — even erroneously

Risk Amplification for SMBs

If you're a small or mid-sized business, data harvesting doesn't just impact you as a consumer — it can expose your **customers, employees, and brand** to serious risk:

- **Third-party platforms** you use (CRM, HR, scheduling, marketing) may harvest your customer data without your full awareness
- **Free tools or apps** often monetize by selling user data — putting your business relationships at risk
- **Aggregated behavior** from your team's tool usage can leak proprietary insights (e.g., patterns in document access, internal communication timing)
- **Cloud-connected devices** like smart printers or cameras may be logging more than you realize

Worse, if customers discover their data is being harvested via your product, service, or platform — **you are the one they'll hold accountable.**

How Data Harvesting Skews AI Outcomes

Because harvested data is collected in the wild — without consent or context — it is often **noisy, biased, or ethically questionable**. Yet it still feeds powerful AI systems.

Consequences include:

- **Reinforcing stereotypes**: Algorithms learn from biased content and perpetuate harmful narratives
- **Algorithmic redlining**: AI trained on skewed behavioral data may discriminate by race, gender, or income
- **Data laundering**: Once data is harvested and anonymized, it's often resold and reused indefinitely — becoming untraceable and unaccountable
- **Synthetic identity risk**: Combined datasets can create shadow profiles or be used to impersonate individuals in fraud or scam scenarios

What begins as "just browsing" becomes **training fuel for systems that make real decisions about people's lives.**

Tactical Checklist: How to Protect Yourself and Your Organization

You can't stop data harvesting everywhere. But you can **reduce your exposure, set stronger boundaries, and demand better standards** from the tools you use.

Checklist for Families and Businesses:

- ☐ Audit all apps, platforms, and devices for passive data collection
- ☐ Delete or disable unused apps — especially those with location or microphone access
- ☐ Use privacy browsers and search engines (e.g., Brave, DuckDuckGo)
- ☐ Block third-party cookies and ad trackers by default
- ☐ Monitor your data footprint with services like Apple's App Privacy Report
- ☐ Read the fine print: What data is collected, why, and with whom is it shared?

- ☐ For SMBs: Review vendor data practices and ask tough questions before integration
- ☐ Avoid free tools unless you fully understand the tradeoff (if it's free, **you** are the product)
- ☐ Teach your team to recognize data-hungry designs and dark patterns
- ☐ Establish internal data hygiene policies to avoid accidental exposure or over-collection

The Business Case for Ethical Data Stewardship

Data harvesting isn't just a privacy issue. It's a **trust issue** — and trust is a strategic asset.

Businesses that prioritize ethical data handling gain:

- Stronger customer loyalty
- Higher employee trust and engagement
- Reduced risk of regulatory fines or legal exposure
- Better vendor partnerships
- Stronger internal AI models (when built with quality, consent-based data)

The message is simple: **Stop feeding AI with data you didn't earn.** Your reputation, your compliance posture, and your future innovation depend on it.

How Biased Data Creates Real-World Injustice

Artificial intelligence doesn't have opinions, agendas, or emotions. It doesn't "see" race, gender, or social class the way people do. But that doesn't mean it's neutral.

AI learns to make decisions by analyzing patterns in historical data — data that is often riddled with the biases of the societies, institutions, and human decisions that produced it. And when those biases go unchecked, AI doesn't just reflect them — **it automates them**.

Biased data transforms inequality into code. It makes discrimination scalable. And it can embed injustice into decisions about hiring, healthcare, housing, education, credit, criminal justice, and more — often without anyone realizing until it's too late.

In a world increasingly run by algorithms, **bad data becomes a civil rights issue.** For business leaders, policymakers, and technologists alike, understanding how data bias works — and how to stop it — is now a moral and operational imperative.

What Is Biased Data?

Data bias occurs when the information used to train an AI system is skewed, incomplete, or unrepresentative in a way that creates **unfair or harmful outcomes**.

Types of bias in AI training data include:

- **Historical bias**: The data reflects past discrimination (e.g., hiring records that favor men)
- **Representation bias**: Some groups are underrepresented or completely missing
- **Measurement bias**: The variables being measured don't capture what they're supposed to (e.g., using zip code as a proxy for creditworthiness)
- **Labeling bias**: Human annotators apply their own prejudices when tagging or scoring data
- **Aggregation bias**: Group-level patterns are treated as universal truths for individuals

These biases are often unintentional. But once they're baked into the model, they become **hard to detect and even harder to remove** — especially when decisions are made at scale.

Real-World Example: Hiring Algorithm Penalizes Women

What Happened

A global tech company deployed an AI recruitment tool to help identify top job applicants. The system was trained on ten years of historical hiring data — resumes from previous successful candidates.

What Went Wrong

Because the company had historically hired mostly men in technical roles, the AI learned to **downgrade resumes that included references to women's colleges or activities (like "women's chess club").** It also favored language patterns more common in male resumes.

What We Learn

Even though gender was never explicitly included as a data point, **the model learned to discriminate** based on proxy indicators — all inherited from biased historical data. The result? Qualified female candidates were systematically deprioritized without any human review.

The Automation of Discrimination

AI systems are increasingly used to make decisions with high stakes — decisions that shape people's futures and freedoms. When these systems are trained on biased data, **they don't just mirror existing inequalities. They institutionalize them.**

Examples of biased AI in the real world:

Domain	AI Use Case	Injustice Created
Criminal Justice	Predictive policing & recidivism scoring	Over-policing of minority communities based on flawed arrest data
Finance	Loan approval and credit scoring	Lower credit limits or denials for people in disadvantaged areas
Healthcare	Risk stratification and treatment prioritization	Underserved populations flagged as lower-risk due to cost bias
Education	Adaptive learning platforms and admissions	Systems reinforce socioeconomic gaps and algorithmic gatekeeping
Housing	Tenant screening and mortgage automation	Redlining patterns reproduced via data proxies like zip codes

These aren't edge cases. They are **systemic failures** — made worse by the illusion that "technology is impartial."

Why Bias Often Goes Undetected

Part of the danger is that biased AI systems **don't always look broken.** They deliver "consistent," "data-driven" results. But those results can be devastating if no one is auditing the inputs or testing for disparate impact.

Reasons bias stays hidden:

- **AI decisions are opaque**: Even developers can't always explain why a model made a specific prediction
- **Proxy variables mask bias**: Age, zip code, education level can act as stand-ins for race or gender
- **No ground truth exists**: For many problems (like who is "high risk" or "qualified"), the label is subjective

- **Success is defined by correlation**: If a model is "accurate," it may still be unfair — and no one checks

Without **transparency, accountability, and regular impact assessment**, AI systems can quietly replicate injustice for years before anyone notices — and by then, the damage is widespread.

The Business Risk of Biased AI

For small and mid-sized organizations, biased AI may seem like someone else's problem — something for big tech or government to solve. But that's a dangerous assumption.

If your company uses AI for:

- Recruiting or candidate screening
- Customer profiling
- Loan or insurance decisions
- Content recommendation
- Fraud detection
- Chatbot or assistant responses
- Predictive analytics for pricing or retention

…then you are already **at risk of deploying bias at scale** — whether you built the system or licensed it.

The consequences can include:

- **Legal exposure** under anti-discrimination or privacy laws
- **Reputational damage** from algorithmic harm or public backlash
- **Customer churn** driven by unfair treatment or misaligned values
- **Lost talent** when biased systems screen out diverse candidates
- **Ineffective models** that underperform because they weren't trained fairly

Bias isn't just an ethics issue. It's an operational liability.

Tactical Steps to Reduce Bias in AI Systems

You don't need to be a data scientist to start building **bias awareness into your AI strategy.** Even basic steps can dramatically reduce risk.

For SMBs Using AI-Powered Platforms

- ☐ Ask vendors how their models were trained — and what bias mitigation steps were taken
- ☐ Require documentation on data sources, diversity audits, and known limitations
- ☐ Test tools on edge cases and minority groups in your user base
- ☐ Don't treat model outputs as gospel — use them to inform human judgment, not replace it
- ☐ Monitor for disparate outcomes over time and escalate anomalies

For Internal Teams Working With AI

- ☐ Review training data for gaps in representation
- ☐ Involve diverse stakeholders in data labeling and model evaluation
- ☐ Use bias detection tools (like IBM AI Fairness 360, Fairlearn, etc.) during development
- ☐ Avoid using sensitive attributes (or proxies) unless legally and ethically justified
- ☐ Establish a bias review checkpoint before deployment — not after

Cultural Shifts to Build Into Your Organization

- Treat fairness as a measurable outcome, not a vague goal
- Encourage team members to speak up when they spot biased patterns
- Build diverse teams that can recognize blind spots early
- Define what "fairness" means in your business context — it may vary by industry
- Be transparent with users: explain what your AI does, what data it uses, and how they can appeal or contest decisions

What "Fixing" Bias Really Means

You can't just "debias the data" and move on. Fixing bias requires **constant, intentional, and human-centered oversight.**

- It means challenging the assumption that historical data reflects acceptable norms
- It means designing systems that are not just accurate, but **equitable**
- It means asking who benefits from each decision — and who might be harmed
- And it means recognizing that in many cases, **the right answer is not to automate at all**

Some decisions are too consequential — or too context-sensitive — to be made by pattern recognition alone.

Data Breaches in the Age of Machine Learning

In the early days of cybersecurity, data breaches were relatively blunt-force affairs: someone broke into a system, stole a database, and vanished with the contents. Today, the game has changed. Data breaches have evolved into **strategic, AI-enabled operations** that use machine learning to find, exploit, and extract sensitive information faster — and more quietly — than ever before.

At the same time, the stakes are higher. The kinds of data being stored, shared, and processed now go far beyond usernames and passwords. We're talking about biometric profiles, location histories, behavioral logs, training data for AI models, and even real-time operational telemetry — all of which can be **weaponized** once in the wrong hands.

For business leaders, especially in small and mid-sized enterprises, the age of machine learning means one thing: **your data is more valuable, more vulnerable, and more actively targeted than ever before.**

Why Machine Learning Has Changed the Breach Landscape

Machine learning — especially when used by cybercriminals — has made data breaches faster, stealthier, and more adaptive. These aren't just smarter attacks; they're **automated, learning systems** that evolve with every attempt.

How Machine Learning Powers Modern Cyber Attacks:

- **Anomaly detection in reverse**: Just as defenders use ML to detect unusual behavior, attackers now use it to **mimic normal activity**, staying under the radar
- **Credential stuffing and brute force automation**: ML models quickly learn which credentials are most likely to succeed across reused accounts
- **Social engineering personalization**: AI scans breached data to craft highly targeted phishing and pretexting campaigns
- **Malware evasion**: Machine learning helps malware dynamically adjust its behavior to avoid endpoint detection

- **Prioritizing soft targets**: AI models evaluate your public-facing systems, rank them by exploitable weaknesses, and adapt attack strategies in real time

The result? A new generation of breaches that are **harder to spot and faster to execute.** And they're increasingly aimed at the "middle market," where defenses are weaker and data is often just as valuable.

Real-World Example: MOVEit Transfer Breach (2023)

What Happened

Progress Software's MOVEit Transfer tool — widely used for secure file transfers — was exploited by a criminal group using an SQL injection vulnerability. But what made this breach different was the **scale and automation** of the attack.

The attackers used machine learning to:

- Automatically scan the internet for exposed MOVEit instances
- Exfiltrate sensitive data using scripted processes
- Filter and classify stolen data for extortion value
- Tailor ransom demands based on the victim's industry, size, and public profile

What Went Wrong

Many organizations had **trusted third-party platforms** to manage their sensitive files without monitoring how they were being updated or exposed. The attackers bypassed traditional detection tools by mimicking normal admin activity.

What We Learn

Modern breaches aren't just technical failures — they're failures of **visibility, automation readiness, and trust in unseen systems.** ML gives attackers the power to act at scale — and they're using it.

The New Data That's Being Breached

Historically, breaches targeted structured data: names, emails, passwords, payment cards. That's still happening — but **today's attackers are going after deeper, richer, and more sensitive targets** that power AI systems and business operations.

High-Value Targets in the Machine Learning Era:

- **AI training datasets**: Includes proprietary customer data, medical records, internal communications, and more
- **ML model files**: Stolen models can be reverse-engineered, poisoned, or sold to competitors
- **Telemetry and usage logs**: Valuable for understanding how internal systems work and what users are doing
- **Voice, video, and biometric archives**: Often stored for personalization, now usable for deepfakes or identity fraud
- **API keys and access tokens**: Grant backdoor access to services integrated across the business
- **Sensor and IoT data**: Including location, environmental inputs, and physical movement — which can reveal operational secrets
- **Synthetic or anonymized data**: Frequently not as anonymous as believed — ML models can often re-identify individuals from patterns

The question isn't just "what happens if this data is stolen?" It's **"what can a machine do with it that a human couldn't?"**

How AI Makes Post-Breach Damage Worse

Once data is stolen, machine learning can make its **exploitation more damaging, more precise, and more profitable**:

- **Automated extortion**: Threat actors use NLP (natural language processing) to tailor ransom notes and leak threats
- **Victim profiling**: Stolen data is cross-referenced with other leaks to identify the most valuable targets
- **Real-time impersonation**: Deepfakes, voice clones, and fake emails use breached data to fool employees or partners
- **Training malicious AI**: Stolen customer service logs, internal chat data, or healthcare records can be used to train new scam bots or disinformation engines
- **Supply chain exploitation**: Access to one company's data often enables attacks on their vendors, clients, or partners

In short, **the breach isn't the end. It's the beginning of a much larger threat cycle** — fueled by automation and scale.

Why SMBs Are Prime Targets

Many SMBs believe they're too small to be targeted. But in the machine learning era, **it's not about who you are — it's about what data you hold** and how well-defended you are.

Reasons attackers love SMBs:

- More likely to use third-party tools with weak security
- Less likely to monitor or patch AI integrations and APIs
- Often store sensitive data in "temporary" places (e.g., spreadsheets, Slack, shared folders)
- Rarely have a full-time security team or proper incident response plan

- Are frequently connected to larger firms through supply chains or vendor ecosystems

Once breached, SMBs are less able to recover — and more likely to pay ransom to avoid operational collapse.

Tactical Steps to Secure Your Data in an ML-Powered World

You can't stop attackers from using machine learning — but you can make your environment **a much harder target**.

Executive-Ready Checklist:

☐ **Map your sensitive data** — including training data, logs, AI models, and device telemetry

☐ **Limit access** to AI tools and datasets using least privilege principles

☐ **Encrypt everything** — not just in transit, but at rest (including ML model files)

☐ **Audit third-party platforms** for data handling, breach history, and AI integrations

☐ **Use behavioral monitoring** to detect subtle data access patterns (insider threats, lateral movement)

☐ **Segment networks** to prevent lateral breach propagation across AI workloads

☐ **Apply model-level protections**: obfuscation, watermarking, and usage monitoring

☐ **Update incident response plans** to include AI-specific breach scenarios (e.g., stolen training data or compromised model integrity)

Invest in AI-Resilient Cyber Hygiene

Modern cyber defense is no longer just about firewalls and antivirus software. It's about **making sure your data and machine learning systems can't be silently exploited.**

Core practices include:

- **Regularly retrain and validate your own AI models** to detect tampering or data drift
- **Log and monitor all AI-related data access** — who touched what, when, and why
- **Perform red team simulations** that assume AI-enabled attackers, not just manual ones
- **Set governance rules for AI output logs** — who stores them, how long, and where
- **Avoid unnecessary data hoarding** — the more you store, the more you risk

Final Thought: If You Train It, You Must Protect It

Every AI initiative inside your company — from a chatbot to a customer segmentation engine — creates **new high-value assets and new high-value targets**. If you're training models, collecting telemetry, or deploying AI for operations, **you are managing a data-rich attack surface.**

Protecting your models, training data, and supporting infrastructure isn't optional. It's **core to your business continuity, brand integrity, and customer trust.**

Because in the machine learning age, **a breach doesn't just steal your data. It steals the intelligence your business runs on.**

Protecting the Data Lifecycle from Collection to Deletion

In the age of AI, data isn't just fuel — it's **infrastructure.** Every model, recommendation, automation, and insight is built on the data your organization collects, processes, stores, and eventually deletes. But if any stage of that lifecycle is exposed or mismanaged, it becomes a **liability** — one that attackers, regulators, and customers are all watching closely.

For small and mid-sized businesses, protecting the full data lifecycle is no longer a luxury or a checkbox. It's an operational imperative. Especially now, as AI systems ingest vast datasets from across your business — often without clear oversight — the risk landscape has shifted.

Protecting your data is protecting your decisions.

This section maps out how to secure the entire data lifecycle — from initial collection to safe deletion — with real-world guardrails, practical best practices, and a clear understanding of what can go wrong at each stage.

What Is the Data Lifecycle?

The **data lifecycle** refers to the end-to-end journey of your information assets — from the moment they're generated or collected to the moment they're securely erased or archived. AI models and analytics platforms depend on this data at nearly every step, making lifecycle security not just a privacy issue, but a business-critical control.

Six Core Stages of the Data Lifecycle:

1. **Collection** — Data is acquired from users, devices, apps, or integrations
2. **Storage** — Data is stored in databases, data lakes, cloud drives, or edge devices
3. **Access & Use** — Data is queried, viewed, transformed, or used in applications and models
4. **Sharing** — Data is transferred internally, externally, or between systems/APIs
5. **Retention** — Data is retained for analysis, compliance, or business needs
6. **Deletion or Archival** — Data is securely disposed of, anonymized, or archived for long-term storage

At every one of these stages, security failures can compromise **customer trust, regulatory compliance, AI reliability, and your brand reputation.**

Stage 1: Collection — Where Consent and Control Begin

This is where your data governance posture is defined. Poor collection practices lead to toxic data lakes, customer mistrust, and privacy violations.

Key Risks:

- Overcollection: Gathering more data than you need — increasing liability
- Ambiguous consent: Users unaware their data will be used to train AI or shared with vendors
- Hidden collection: Passive data harvesting (e.g., click tracking, device metadata)
- Biased input: Data that reflects skewed samples or unjustified assumptions

Tactical Best Practices:

- ☐ Collect only the data you truly need — nothing more
- ☐ Use **plain-language consent** that explains how and why data is used
- ☐ Tag data at the moment of collection with purpose, owner, and sensitivity classification
- ☐ Avoid "default on" tracking or behavior logging without clear user opt-in
- ☐ Establish different protocols for personal, sensitive, and anonymous data

Pro Tip: If you can't clearly explain why you're collecting a data point — and how it supports business goals — you shouldn't be collecting it.

Stage 2: Storage — Don't Let Data Decay Into Risk

Data storage is where most breaches originate. Attackers aren't looking to intercept data in transit — they're looking for **insecure, forgotten, or misconfigured stores** where valuable data is sitting idle and unmonitored.

Key Risks:

- Misconfigured cloud buckets (e.g., S3, Azure Blob) left open to the internet
- Unencrypted databases or backups
- Storage of raw AI training data without access control
- Stale data retained long after its usefulness ends
- Lack of metadata or audit trails for who accessed what and when

Tactical Best Practices:

- ☐ Encrypt all sensitive data — both at rest and in transit
- ☐ Use data classification to separate highly sensitive data from general records
- ☐ Tag AI training data with source, sensitivity, and expiration timelines
- ☐ Limit access using role-based permissions (not everyone needs everything)
- ☐ Regularly review and audit cloud storage permissions
- ☐ Implement immutability where appropriate (e.g., audit logs, financial records)

Pro Tip: Assume every data store will be breached eventually. Design storage with **containment and isolation** in mind.

Stage 3: Access and Use — Where Most Mistakes Happen

The more powerful your AI tools and dashboards, the more tempting it is for employees — or contractors — to explore or manipulate data **outside of policy.** This is the riskiest phase for accidental exposure, overreach, or insider threats.

Key Risks:

- Overly broad access to sensitive data or model inputs
- Use of production data in development or testing environments
- Insecure AI prompts that leak private data
- No monitoring of user behavior or unusual queries
- Model drift or hallucinations exposing sensitive training content

Tactical Best Practices:

- ☐ Implement "least privilege" access to all datasets and interfaces
- ☐ Monitor and log all access to sensitive data and models
- ☐ Ban use of production data in dev/test unless anonymized or sandboxed
- ☐ Track model output — especially for sensitive domains — for privacy leakage
- ☐ Train staff to recognize privacy violations in prompt-based AI tools (e.g., chatbots, assistants)

Pro Tip: Every AI interaction is a potential data leak — **especially when the model is trained on your internal content.**

Stage 4: Sharing — Where Trust Gets Transferred

Whether via APIs, vendor integrations, or exported reports, data sharing is often where **controls break down.** Once information leaves your core system, you may lose visibility, protection, and legal standing.

Key Risks:

- Sending PII or regulated data to third parties without clear contracts
- API integrations that lack rate limiting, auth tokens, or encryption
- Shadow IT tools (e.g., file sharing apps, personal accounts)
- Lack of vendor oversight — or unclear data handling in SaaS platforms
- Misuse of shared AI models trained on internal data

Tactical Best Practices:

- ☐ Establish a data sharing policy that defines what can be shared, with whom, and under what terms
- ☐ Use secure APIs with authentication and encryption
- ☐ Require Data Processing Agreements (DPAs) from all vendors
- ☐ Apply data masking, tokenization, or synthetic substitutes where appropriate
- ☐ Maintain logs and real-time monitoring of outbound data flows

Pro Tip: Assume that **any shared data may eventually become public**. Filter accordingly.

Stage 5: Retention — Don't Store What You Can't Protect

Keeping data "just in case" is a common trap — but in an AI environment, **the longer data sits, the more risk it creates.** Retention without purpose increases exposure and adds noise to your systems.

Key Risks:

- Retaining sensitive data past its operational need
- Misaligned legal, operational, and AI training retention schedules
- Failing to offboard datasets after contract terminations or personnel exits
- Keeping data that is inaccurate, stale, or misleading — polluting future models

Tactical Best Practices:

- ☐ Define data retention schedules by category and legal requirement
- ☐ Automatically expire or archive stale datasets
- ☐ Remove access to retained data from inactive accounts or departments
- ☐ Don't train new AI models on outdated or unvetted archives
- ☐ Align HR and IT offboarding with data access termination

Pro Tip: If you can't justify why a dataset is still being retained — **it's time to delete it or archive it securely.**

Stage 6: Deletion — The Final Line of Defense

Data deletion is more than hitting "delete." It's about **secure, auditable, irreversible removal** from all systems — including backups, caches, and AI models. Failure here can create lasting risk — especially under GDPR, CCPA, and similar laws.

Key Risks:

- Data lingering in backups or logs
- Inability to fully remove data from machine learning training sets
- Forgotten copies in offline or shadow systems
- Lack of proof or audit trail for deletion
- Failure to honor user or customer deletion requests

Tactical Best Practices:

- ☐ Use deletion methods that are irreversible and meet industry standards
- ☐ Confirm deletion from all storage tiers, including archives and offsite
- ☐ Use machine unlearning techniques to retrain AI systems if required by law
- ☐ Keep a tamper-proof audit log of all deletions for compliance
- ☐ Respect user deletion requests within legally mandated timeframes

Pro Tip: Deletion isn't just the end of the lifecycle — it's the **final test of your data integrity and trustworthiness.**

Final Thought: Treat Data Like a Living Asset

Data isn't static. It changes, it ages, it loses value, and it creates risk the longer it stays unmonitored. In an AI-driven world, your ability to **control the full lifecycle of your data is a direct reflection of your cybersecurity posture.**

If your organization collects it, stores it, uses it, shares it, or trains on it — **you are responsible for protecting it until the moment it's gone.**

CHAPTER 6

Jobs, Economy, and Human Dignity

Automation and the Threat of Mass Unemployment

The promise of automation has always been increased productivity, lower costs, and freeing humans from repetitive tasks. But as artificial intelligence evolves far beyond assembly lines — into knowledge work, customer service, creative tasks, and even management — that promise has come with a sharp edge: **mass displacement.**

What was once limited to factory jobs is now targeting white-collar roles once thought irreplaceable. And it's not happening in decades. It's happening **now**.

AI-powered automation is not just transforming industries — it's redefining what it means to be *employable*. For small and mid-sized businesses (SMBs), this creates a paradox: how do you reap the benefits of automation without destabilizing your workforce, your values, or your long-term growth?

Let's examine what's real, what's overstated, and how leaders can prepare for a future where **humans and machines don't just coexist — they compete.**

The Shift from Task Automation to Role Automation

Historically, automation was focused on **narrow tasks**: sorting, scanning, moving, calculating. These systems were rule-based, repeatable, and physical.

But AI has unlocked **cognitive automation** — the ability to make decisions, generate language, interpret visual cues, and interact with humans. It's not replacing one task at a time. It's replacing entire roles.

Roles being rapidly disrupted by AI-driven automation:

- Customer service representatives
- Paralegals and contract reviewers
- Bookkeepers and payroll processors
- HR coordinators
- Copywriters and marketing assistants
- Basic coding and QA testers
- Administrative support staff
- Data entry clerks
- Technical support tiers 1 and 2
- Sales development reps (SDRs)

And that's just the beginning. These roles are often the **backbone of SMB operations** — making this not just a workforce issue, but a strategic business risk.

Real-World Example: Major Tech Firm Cuts 10,000 Jobs, Credits AI Efficiency

What Happened

A multinational technology company announced a wave of layoffs, eliminating over 10,000 roles across customer success, recruiting, and marketing.

What Went Right (for efficiency)

The company had invested heavily in generative AI and customer automation platforms. Tasks like support ticket handling, resume screening, and content production were now handled by AI — at scale.

What Went Wrong

The layoffs created internal morale issues, public backlash, and brand damage. Customers began to notice a lack of human nuance in responses. Former employees warned of institutional knowledge loss that would be hard to replace.

What We Learn

Efficiency gains don't equal resilience. Replacing roles too quickly — or without retraining and cultural planning — creates deeper risk. AI isn't just a tech upgrade; it's a workforce disruption.

Why AI Threatens More Jobs Than Previous Automation Waves

Many past automation revolutions (e.g., mechanization, computing, robotics) created new job classes even as they displaced others. But AI may break that pattern. Here's why:

1. It Targets Mental, Not Just Manual Labor

Generative AI and machine learning are attacking roles that were traditionally protected by education, experience, and critical thinking.

2. It Scales at Low Marginal Cost

Unlike a robot that needs manufacturing and maintenance, AI software can be deployed instantly across thousands of roles with minimal overhead.

3. It Feeds on the Knowledge Workers Create

AI learns from the work we do — emails, documents, code, calls — which means it improves by watching humans… and then replaces them using their own output as training data.

4. It Enables Centralized Efficiency

Companies can consolidate roles, departments, or even entire functions under AI management — reducing need for distributed teams.

Common Misconceptions About AI and Employment

To lead with clarity, leaders must separate fear from fact. Let's debunk a few common myths:

Myth 1: "AI will only eliminate low-skill jobs."
Reality: AI is disrupting high-skill, high-paying roles — including lawyers, designers, consultants, and analysts. Job **routine**, not job **status**, determines risk.

Myth 2: "For every job lost, AI will create a new one."
Reality: New roles are being created, but they're **fewer, more specialized, and harder to access** without technical expertise. Many displaced workers won't transition easily.

Myth 3: "People can just be reskilled."
Reality: Reskilling is crucial — but it's slow, expensive, and often doesn't match the pace of displacement. A 50-year-old customer support agent won't become a prompt engineer overnight.

Myth 4: "This won't affect SMBs — only big tech."
Reality: SMBs are already replacing contractors, assistants, and entry-level staff with AI tools. The impact is quieter, but just as real.

Warning Signs Your Organization May Be Heading Toward AI-Led Layoffs

Many businesses begin automating to improve productivity — but gradually edge into workforce reduction without a formal plan. If you see these signs, start preparing for strategic disruption:

- Key roles being partially handled by AI tools (e.g., chatbots, auto-drafting tools)
- Reduced hiring for entry-level positions "due to automation"
- Increasing focus on data collection and process digitization
- Budget cuts justified by "AI efficiency gains"
- New tools replacing existing staff functions without retraining plans
- Lack of transparency about where AI is being used internally

Tactical Best Practices: Ethical and Strategic AI Adoption

It is possible to deploy AI in a way that supports — not replaces — your workforce. But it requires **intentional leadership** and **clear guardrails**.

Executive Readiness Checklist:

☐ **Conduct a workforce impact assessment** before rolling out automation

☐ **Map every AI deployment to the human role it affects** — directly or indirectly

☐ **Create retraining pathways** before displacement begins

☐ **Set ethical automation policies** that define what AI will not be used to replace

☐ **Use AI to augment, not eliminate**, roles where judgment, empathy, or trust are critical

☐ **Be transparent** with employees about where AI is being used — and why

☐ **Set cultural expectations** that value human expertise even in an AI-augmented future

Preparing Employees for an Automated Future

Whether you're an employer or an employee, the rules of value creation are shifting. Skills that used to guarantee job security may no longer be enough.

Most in-demand human skills in an AI-saturated market:

- Strategic judgment
- Emotional intelligence and communication
- Cross-disciplinary thinking
- Ethical reasoning and governance
- Prompt design and AI evaluation (AI literacy)
- Data interpretation and decision framing
- Human-centered design and customer empathy

AI may generate the words, but **humans still decide what matters.**

What SMB leaders should do:

- Launch internal upskilling initiatives (e.g., AI literacy workshops, ethical AI roundtables)
- Promote cross-training between technical and non-technical teams
- Reward employees who improve workflows using AI — without reducing headcount
- Appoint an internal automation ethics lead or committee
- Document changes to responsibilities when AI tools are introduced

The Risk of Doing Nothing

Ignoring the workforce implications of AI is not a neutral choice. It's a **strategic liability** that can trigger:

- Culture degradation and loss of trust
- Unintended layoffs that harm long-term resilience
- Reputational damage in your industry or community
- Talent flight as top performers seek value-aligned companies
- Regulatory scrutiny around AI labor practices and fairness

AI will change your workforce — whether you guide it or not.

Final Thought: Automate with Accountability

The future isn't man *or* machine. It's **managing the machine** — with clarity, fairness, and long-term vision. If AI helps your business do more with less, that's not inherently bad. But if "less" always means **fewer people, lower pay, and more surveillance**, you're trading long-term health for short-term profit.

The real ROI of AI comes from **augmenting human excellence**, not replacing it.

The businesses that win won't be the ones that automate fastest. They'll be the ones that automate **wisely** — with humanity at the center.

The Rise of "Ghost Work" Behind AI Platforms

Artificial intelligence systems are often described as "autonomous," "self-learning," or "fully automated." But behind the curtain of seamless apps, intelligent chatbots, and recommendation engines lies a hidden layer of human labor — millions of people around the world performing tedious, low-paid tasks to keep AI running. This is known as **ghost work**: invisible labor that powers machine intelligence, but receives none of the credit, recognition, or protection.

Ghost workers are not employed by the companies that rely on them. They are contractors, gig workers, or platform-based annotators who perform essential tasks like labeling training data, moderating content, fixing model outputs, or simulating conversations. These workers are the scaffolding of AI systems — yet they operate under precarious conditions, often paid pennies per task, with little transparency or recourse when things go wrong.

For business leaders using AI tools, this raises a difficult but essential question: **Are your AI efficiencies built on exploited labor you never see?**

What Is Ghost Work?

Ghost work refers to the hidden, outsourced human labor required to keep AI systems functioning. This includes:

- Image tagging for computer vision
- Text labeling for natural language models
- Audio transcription and voice segmentation
- Flagging toxic content or misinformation
- Ranking search results or social feeds
- Reviewing chatbot responses for coherence or bias

These tasks are often performed through platforms like Amazon Mechanical Turk, Appen, Scale AI, Remotasks, and others. Workers are distributed across the globe — from the U.S. and Eastern Europe to the Philippines, Kenya, and India — and may be doing this work full-time, part-time, or as a last resort for income.

The irony is sharp: **AI's "intelligence" is often just well-packaged human judgment.**

Real-World Example: Content Moderation Teams at Scale

What Happened
A major social media company outsourced its content moderation to a third-party firm, employing thousands of workers to review disturbing videos, hate speech, and political propaganda. These workers operated under intense pressure, often watching hundreds of flagged posts per shift, with minimal mental health support.

What Went Wrong
Despite doing critical safety work, the moderators were paid low hourly wages, given limited benefits, and worked in psychologically harmful conditions. Several later reported PTSD-like symptoms. The parent company distanced itself from responsibility, citing "contractor status."

What We Learn
Ghost work isn't limited to training AI — it also maintains AI. And when this labor is outsourced without oversight, it creates ethical liabilities and reputational risks that no company can fully wash its hands of.

Why Ghost Work Exists — and Why It's Growing

AI systems rely on data. But raw data is messy, ambiguous, and full of edge cases. To be useful, it must be labeled, categorized, corrected, or filtered — and there is no algorithm that can do this as accurately as a human.

AI also breaks. Chatbots go off-script, image classifiers get confused, content moderation filters miss the mark. Human reviewers step in to correct, retrain, and supervise — often anonymously.

Ghost work is growing for several reasons:

- The demand for training data is exploding
- Enterprises want faster model updates and better accuracy
- AI systems are being deployed in more nuanced, high-stakes environments
- Companies want to appear "automated" while still relying on human fallback
- Outsourcing platforms provide cheap, scalable labor with minimal oversight

For every "automated" insight or response, there may be a chain of invisible workers behind it — labeling, reviewing, or cleaning up what AI cannot handle.

Ethical Concerns for SMBs and Enterprise Buyers

Many businesses adopt AI tools without knowing how they're built or maintained. Vendors rarely disclose where their training data comes from, how it was labeled, or who maintains performance quality post-deployment.

If your business uses AI, you may be inadvertently participating in — or benefiting from — ghost work without realizing it.

Key ethical risks include:

- Use of unvetted or underpaid labor in jurisdictions with weak labor laws
- Exposure to psychologically harmful content by moderators or annotators
- Lack of transparency in how your vendor trains or maintains its models
- Data privacy concerns if annotators are reviewing sensitive user inputs
- Reinforcement of social and economic inequities through exploitative contracts

This isn't just a moral issue — it's a **supply chain risk.** The people who train your AI are part of your extended operational footprint. If they are mistreated, misclassified, or harmed, the consequences can rebound onto your brand.

Tactical Steps to Ensure Ethical AI Supply Chains

You may not control the platforms your AI vendor uses — but you can choose to **demand visibility, set standards, and make ethical procurement part of your governance.**

Checklist for Ethical AI Procurement:

☐ Ask vendors where their training data comes from and how it's labeled
☐ Require disclosures on labor practices and contractor protections
☐ Include ghost work provisions in AI sourcing and compliance reviews
☐ Prefer vendors that employ annotators directly, pay fair wages,

and offer support services

☐ Avoid free or low-cost AI APIs that cannot explain their data or quality processes

☐ Support projects and platforms that are transparent about their human-in-the-loop systems

Pro Tip: Add ghost work accountability to your vendor risk management scorecard — alongside security, privacy, and performance.

The Business Case for Fair AI Labor

Supporting ethical data work is not just altruism — it protects the quality, reliability, and resilience of your AI systems.

Human annotators who are paid fairly, trained properly, and supported emotionally are:

- More accurate and consistent in labeling tasks
- Less likely to rush or manipulate task outcomes for speed
- More invested in understanding edge cases or ambiguities
- Better equipped to flag problems or gaps in model performance

Poor labor conditions produce poor data — and poor data creates weak or dangerous AI.

If your business relies on AI, then **investing in human dignity upstream is a form of risk management.** You are only as strong as the invisible labor you depend on.

Final Thought: Don't Let AI Obscure the Human Cost

Artificial intelligence may reduce headcount, streamline operations, and automate decision-making. But it does not eliminate the need for human insight — it simply **pushes that labor further into the shadows.**

Ghost work isn't going away. But with transparency, ethical sourcing, and responsible oversight, it doesn't have to remain invisible.

Make sure your AI success story doesn't come at the cost of someone else's exploitation.

Economic Inequality Accelerated by AI Monopolies

Artificial intelligence has been hailed as a great equalizer — a force that democratizes knowledge, automates opportunity, and levels the playing field. But in practice, the opposite is often true. The AI economy is increasingly dominated by a handful of corporations with the resources, infrastructure, and access to data needed to train, deploy, and profit from large-scale models. The result? A widening economic gap between tech-rich giants and everyone else.

AI, like the internet before it, has the potential to create new industries and job categories. But unlike the early web, **today's AI breakthroughs are centralized, capital-intensive, and structurally exclusionary.** Small and mid-sized businesses, individuals, and even nations are finding themselves dependent on systems they didn't build, can't fully control, and must pay to access — often under opaque or extractive terms.

This isn't just a technology issue. It's a growing systemic risk to the economy — one that threatens to **entrench inequality, stifle innovation, and concentrate power in ways that democratic societies struggle to regulate.**

How AI Becomes an Inequality Engine

The architecture of AI — particularly large-scale machine learning — favors incumbents. Those with the **most data, most compute, and deepest pockets** enjoy compounding advantages that are increasingly hard to compete with.

Key factors accelerating inequality:

- **Data hoarding**: The best models require massive, proprietary datasets — something only large platforms can collect at scale
- **Compute monopolies**: Training frontier AI models requires enormous processing power, often available only through cloud giants or national labs
- **Talent drain**: The top AI researchers are recruited (and overpaid) by a small set of firms, creating a knowledge moat
- **Vertical integration**: The same firms build the models, own the platforms, sell the APIs, and shape the standards
- **Pay-to-play APIs**: Smaller companies must license access to AI — paying usage fees to firms that benefit from their data, their traffic, and their customers

This creates a flywheel: the more these companies operate at scale, the more data and profit they accumulate, reinforcing their dominance.

Real-World Example: Small Publisher Disrupted by AI Aggregation

What Happened
A regional news publisher discovered its original articles were being summarized, paraphrased, and surfaced by AI-driven content platforms — with zero attribution. These platforms used the publisher's RSS feeds and public web pages to train models and generate near-duplicate content that ranked higher in search results.

What Went Wrong
Traffic plummeted. Ad revenue collapsed. Attempts to challenge the scraping were met with vague legal language about "fair use" and model training exemptions. The publisher had no realistic path to enforce rights or demand compensation.

What We Learn
When AI platforms absorb the work of smaller creators — without payment or permission — they extract value **without returning it.** The result is a power imbalance where those who *generate* knowledge are undercut by those who *synthesize* it.

The Rise of AI Rentier Capitalism

Many AI companies no longer aim to sell tools — they aim to **own infrastructure.** That means controlling the systems others must pay to access, regardless of whether they're creating, consuming, or competing.

Examples of this model include:

- Charging per API call for access to general-purpose language models
- Embedding AI into office suites or customer tools, locking users into paid subscriptions
- Licensing models trained on public data without compensating contributors
- Imposing restrictive terms that prevent users from fine-tuning or self-hosting
- Bundling AI into platforms that displace independent vendors and apps

This dynamic mirrors other monopolistic trends — cloud computing, app stores, gig platforms — but with a twist: **the underlying intelligence itself becomes the toll booth.**

Instead of building and competing, smaller players become **perpetual renters in someone else's digital city.**

Economic Implications for SMBs and Local Economies

The implications of AI monopolies extend beyond Silicon Valley. They ripple into:

- **Retail and e-commerce**: AI-driven ad targeting and recommendation algorithms now require platform integration, often at unsustainable ad costs
- **Marketing and content creation**: Generative AI tools replace freelance and agency work, consolidating creative services under centralized models
- **Customer support**: SMBs must choose between expensive AI support systems or inferior service quality — while large firms deploy custom LLMs
- **Healthcare and finance**: Predictive AI tools are increasingly licensed from mega-platforms, with little ability for SMBs to compete on outcomes or affordability
- **Hiring and HR tech**: Algorithmic screening tools favor data-rich, model-trained systems that are too expensive or opaque for smaller employers

This tilts markets. **Big firms get smarter, faster, and cheaper. Small firms fall behind — not for lack of skill or ambition, but because the infrastructure of intelligence is no longer neutral.**

The Global Divide: AI Colonialism and the South-North Split

Beyond companies, **entire countries are at risk of being left behind**. Most frontier AI models are trained in the U.S., China, and parts of the EU. Nations without massive cloud access, elite technical talent, or English-language dominance find themselves **consuming** AI, not creating it.

This leads to:

- Economic dependence on imported software
- Cultural erasure when local languages, norms, and values are excluded from training data
- Loss of innovation as domestic industries rely on foreign models
- Vulnerability to surveillance or influence via embedded AI systems in infrastructure

Some have called this "AI colonialism": the idea that digital intelligence — like natural resources before it — is being extracted from many to benefit a few.

Tactical Best Practices: How to Compete Without Capitulating

SMBs and emerging economies may not be able to outspend tech giants, but they can still navigate the AI economy with clarity, autonomy, and strategic focus.

Ways to operate in an unequal AI environment:

☐ **Audit your AI dependencies** — know which vendors, platforms, and APIs you rely on and what power they hold over pricing, access, or IP

☐ **Invest in internal data** — your own customer, product, and operational data can be a differentiator if properly protected and modeled

☐ **Use open-source AI where feasible** — consider local models (e.g., LLaMA, Mistral, Falcon) to reduce reliance on proprietary systems

☐ **Diversify vendors** — avoid concentration in a single AI or cloud provider to reduce future lock-in

☐ **Demand transparency from AI tools** — ask about training data, model limitations, and content sourcing

☐ **Build for niche markets** — focus on sectors or use cases too specific or complex for general-purpose AI to dominate

☐ **Collaborate with other SMBs** — pool resources to build shared data models or negotiate with vendors as a collective

Policy and Leadership Responses to Watch

There is growing awareness — even at the regulatory level — of AI's monopolistic tendencies. Several initiatives are worth monitoring:

- The EU's **Digital Markets Act** and **AI Act**, which aim to curb platform dominance and ensure fair competition
- The U.S. Federal Trade Commission (FTC) investigations into AI transparency and anticompetitive behavior
- UN and OECD frameworks calling for global equity in AI development and deployment
- Local government initiatives supporting small business access to AI infrastructure and education
- Open-source alliances forming to provide alternatives to closed, corporate models

But policy alone won't close the gap. Businesses must make deliberate choices to **retain agency in an ecosystem increasingly tilted toward centralization.**

Final Thought: Don't Just Use AI — Own Your Position In It

Artificial intelligence has the potential to unlock massive value — but that value is not distributed equally. Without deliberate design, AI becomes a **concentration engine**, rewarding those with scale, infrastructure, and access, while leaving others dependent and displaced.

For business leaders and policymakers, the goal isn't to halt progress — it's to **reclaim participation**. To ensure that AI is not just a product we rent, but a capability we shape. That means investing in transparency, ethics, and autonomy — and refusing to accept a future where innovation belongs only to those who can afford to monopolize it.

Protecting Human Dignity in a Machine-Driven Economy

The advance of artificial intelligence has triggered a wave of automation, algorithmic decision-making, and digital transformation across every sector. For many, this promises efficiency, scale, and insight. But behind the dashboards and models lies a more human question: **What happens to dignity when machines start deciding what people are worth?**

In an economy increasingly optimized by software, **human dignity is at risk of being reduced to performance metrics, behavioral patterns, and predictive scores.** When AI dictates who gets hired, who gets approved, who gets heard, or who gets ignored — the stakes go far beyond productivity.

For business leaders, this isn't a philosophical debate. It's a real-world responsibility. As companies adopt machine-driven systems to manage people, processes, and profits, they must also protect **what makes work — and decision-making — fundamentally human.**

This means ensuring that **efficiency doesn't eclipse empathy**, and that AI is used to elevate human contribution — not erase or degrade it.

What Is Human Dignity in the AI Era?

Dignity, in this context, refers to **the right of individuals to be treated with respect, fairness, and agency — regardless of whether a machine is involved.**

In a machine-driven economy, dignity means:

- Being **seen as more than data** — not reduced to an algorithmic profile
- Having the **right to know** how decisions that affect you are made
- Being able to **contest or appeal** automated outcomes
- Not being displaced, surveilled, or manipulated without cause or consent
- Having your **skills, experience, and humanity valued**, even in the presence of superior automation

When dignity erodes, organizations don't just suffer moral failure — they face legal, cultural, and reputational risk. Employees disengage. Customers defect. Talent avoids you. And the systems you trust begin to undermine the people they were meant to serve.

Real-World Example: Algorithmic Firing Without Human Review

What Happened
A major e-commerce platform deployed AI systems to monitor warehouse productivity. Workers were automatically flagged for termination if their scan rates fell below a certain threshold — regardless of illness, injury, or shift conditions.

What Went Wrong
Dozens of workers reported being fired via app notifications or emails, without any human contact. Some were let go despite years

of high performance. There was no formal appeals process — only a system-generated explanation based on output statistics.

What We Learn
Automated systems can dehumanize people quickly when there's no buffer, context, or compassion. Even accurate metrics become unjust when **used in isolation** — without space for dignity, due process, or dialogue.

Where Dignity Is at Risk in the Business Workflow

You don't need to fire people by algorithm to risk dehumanization. Many everyday AI deployments create subtle — but significant — threats to human dignity:

- **AI recruiting systems** that ghost applicants or auto-reject based on profile keywords
- **Sales and marketing automation** that manipulates emotion or attention without disclosure
- **Employee surveillance tools** that track keystrokes, webcams, or behavior without consent
- **Performance dashboards** that reduce people to red/yellow/green status indicators
- **Content filters or chatbots** that make users feel unheard or miscategorized
- **AI advisors or tools** that dismiss customer complexity in favor of scripted responses
- **Decision automation systems** (e.g., credit, healthcare, insurance) that deny access with no explanation

These tools may be efficient. But without proper governance, they risk turning people into **inputs, risks, or errors** — rather than individuals deserving fairness and respect.

Practical Principles for Human-Centered AI Deployment

To protect dignity in a machine-optimized world, companies need a framework that prioritizes **respect, transparency, and agency.** This doesn't require slowing down innovation — it requires applying intention and oversight.

The Three Pillars of Dignity-Centered AI

1. Transparency
People must know when they're being evaluated, scored, or filtered by an algorithm — and why.

- Notify users when decisions are automated
- Provide explanations or context for decisions, not just outcomes
- Disclose data sources and modeling assumptions where possible

2. Contestability
People must be able to question, appeal, or seek redress for decisions that impact them.

- Offer clear processes to dispute or escalate automated decisions
- Ensure a human is available to review contested outcomes
- Log all decisions and provide access to affected individuals upon request

3. Inclusion
AI must be designed to serve diverse populations — not just average users or ideal customers.

- Involve stakeholders from multiple backgrounds in design and testing

- Evaluate models for fairness across race, gender, age, ability, and culture
- Consider the edge cases — not just the statistical majority

Executive Action Checklist: Embedding Dignity into AI Strategy

This is not a technical problem — it's a leadership one. Your organization's values are expressed not just in your mission statement, but in how your systems treat people when no one's watching.

☐ Appoint an **AI Ethics Lead** or working group responsible for dignity-related impact reviews

☐ Require **human oversight** in all high-stakes decision systems (e.g., hiring, discipline, denial of service)

☐ Ban fully automated termination or rejection processes

☐ Conduct regular **"dignity audits"**: How do your systems treat users, customers, applicants, and staff?

☐ Engage frontline employees and customers in AI feedback loops

☐ Publish **AI use disclosures** on your website or product pages

☐ Train leadership to recognize dignity risk as **brand and operational risk**

Why This Matters for Small and Mid-Sized Businesses

It may seem like an issue for big tech or global platforms, but the **impacts of dignity loss are felt fastest in smaller organizations.** One automated email, one insensitive system message, or one AI-generated mistake can destroy a customer relationship or employee trust — especially when you lack the PR muscle to recover quickly.

On the flip side, **embedding dignity into your AI strategy can be a differentiator.**

- Customers feel respected and return
- Employees stay longer and perform better
- Regulators view you as proactive, not reactive
- Vendors and partners trust your data governance
- Your brand stands for more than just "digital transformation"

In a machine-driven world, **being human becomes a competitive advantage.**

Final Thought: Let Machines Optimize — But Let Humans Lead

AI can be an extraordinary tool — for productivity, prediction, insight, and innovation. But it must remain **a tool.** When it replaces judgment with metrics, removes empathy from process, or puts automation ahead of accountability, it erodes the very fabric of your organization.

Leadership in the age of AI means more than upgrading systems. It means **upholding standards.** It means knowing when to trust the model — and when to intervene on behalf of the people the model can't see.

Protecting human dignity isn't about resisting progress. It's about ensuring that **as machines get smarter, we don't get colder.**

Policies and Retraining Programs That Can Bridge the Gap

As AI-driven transformation accelerates, the most critical bottleneck isn't technology — it's people. Automation is replacing or reshaping millions of jobs across industries. But very few organizations have a clear, structured response to the workforce disruption it's causing.

For businesses — especially small and mid-sized enterprises — the challenge isn't just deciding **whether** to adopt AI. It's deciding how to adopt it **without leaving your team behind.** That means building policies, programs, and cultures that help employees shift roles, learn new skills, and contribute to the future, not just survive it.

Governments and large corporations may talk about "reskilling at scale," but for most leaders, the real work happens inside the business. **Are you creating a bridge — or a cliff — between the present and the future of work?**

The Retraining Imperative: Why It Can't Wait

AI and automation are already eliminating or reconfiguring roles in:

- Customer service
- Marketing and sales ops
- Logistics and supply chain
- Finance and accounting
- HR and recruiting
- Legal review and compliance
- Administrative support
- Manufacturing and field services

What's changing isn't just tools — it's **core job functions**. Without structured retraining, many employees will face one of two options: early exit or forced obsolescence. Neither outcome supports resilience, retention, or continuity.

Retraining is no longer a perk. It's a strategic requirement.

Real-World Example: Retail Chain Creates Internal AI Academy

What Happened
A large regional retailer anticipated that automation would eliminate over 1,000 back-office roles within two years. Instead of laying off affected staff, leadership partnered with a local college and tech firm to create an "AI Academy" — offering part-time, paid training in data handling, prompt design, analytics, and model supervision.

What Went Right
Over 400 employees moved into newly created roles in digital operations, customer intelligence, and supply chain optimization. Turnover dropped. Internal mobility rose. Former inventory clerks became model monitors. Call center staff were retrained as chatbot trainers.

What We Learn
Retraining doesn't have to mean starting from scratch. With the right support, **existing employees can become your most valuable AI collaborators.**

Core Policy Areas for Bridging the AI Skills Gap

Bridging the workforce gap caused by AI requires **policy shifts, not just training modules.** Leaders must embed workforce transition into how the organization hires, promotes, measures, and governs change.

1. Workforce Impact Assessments

Before deploying automation, conduct structured evaluations of how each tool will affect current roles.

Policy Checklist:

☐ Require an AI impact assessment for every new system
☐ Identify which roles will be automated, augmented, or displaced
☐ Involve affected departments early in the planning phase
☐ Quantify retraining needs before deployment
☐ Report findings to executive leadership or a governance committee

2. Reskilling Mandates

Make retraining part of the transformation budget — not an afterthought.

Policy Checklist:

☐ Allocate a percentage of AI savings to reskilling (e.g., 10–15%)
☐ Offer learning stipends or internal "reskill tracks" tied to automation roadmaps
☐ Create a company-wide expectation that AI changes are paired with human enablement
☐ Make retraining participation part of performance development, not just recovery

3. Role Transition Pathways

Don't just teach skills — build clear bridges from one role to another.

Policy Checklist:

☐ Map redundant roles to emerging needs (e.g., from receptionist to AI onboarding concierge)
☐ Publish job transition paths with example salaries and role expectations
☐ Pair retraining with mentoring from current employees in target functions
☐ Guarantee interview opportunities for retrained internal candidates
☐ Offer voluntary early transitions before job elimination occurs

4. AI Literacy for All

Regardless of role or department, everyone should understand how AI works — and how to work with it.

Policy Checklist:

☐ Offer quarterly "AI 101" workshops for all staff
☐ Require basic AI literacy training for managers, HR, and team leads
☐ Create accessible internal resources explaining your AI tools, policies, and risks
☐ Include AI awareness in onboarding and compliance training
☐ Provide business-focused primers on terms like LLM, model drift, hallucination, and bias

5. Ethical Employment Commitments

Make it clear — in writing — that your company won't use AI as a shortcut to cut corners or people.

Policy Checklist:

☐ Publish a statement of ethical AI labor use
☐ Prohibit fully automated firings or reductions without human review
☐ Set internal hiring goals for AI-augmented roles
☐ Track equity metrics to ensure retraining access isn't skewed
☐ Protect wages and benefits for transitioning employees

What Skills Are Worth Developing?

Retraining doesn't mean everyone becomes a coder. The majority of high-value future roles will be **hybrid human-AI roles** — where judgment, collaboration, and design matter more than syntax.

Key Skills for the Machine-Augmented Workforce

- **Prompt design**: Writing, refining, and testing inputs for generative AI tools
- **AI system supervision**: Reviewing outputs, catching errors, escalating risks
- **Data fluency**: Understanding how to read, interpret, and challenge AI-driven metrics
- **Process redesign**: Reimagining workflows to incorporate intelligent tools
- **Ethical reasoning**: Applying fairness and safety principles in automated contexts
- **AI communication**: Explaining AI decisions or tools to non-technical users
- **Tool integration**: Connecting no-code or low-code solutions into operations

Every department — from finance to HR to customer service — will need these skills in some form.

Funding and Support Models That Work

Even small businesses can implement high-impact retraining by **partnering smartly and budgeting early.**

Ideas to consider:

- **Local education partnerships**: Collaborate with community colleges or workforce boards
- **Internal bootcamps**: Create 6- to 12-week guided learning cohorts for AI roles
- **Cross-training exchanges**: Let employees shadow teams that already use automation
- **Micro-certifications**: Offer recognition for mastering narrow but critical skills
- **External funding**: Tap into public grants or AI-focused economic development programs
- **Shared vendor training**: Ask your AI providers to co-create role-specific training for your staff

Retraining as Cultural Transformation

The most successful retraining efforts aren't just about skills — they're about **identity.** When employees see AI as a threat, they resist it. But when they see it as a path to growth — and when leadership backs that vision — everything changes.

Ways to reinforce a reskilling culture:

- Celebrate internal success stories in newsletters or town halls
- Recognize AI-literate teams with awards or incentives
- Use automation wins to fund career development programs
- Train managers to coach, not just manage, through transitions

- Emphasize dignity and career evolution — not "efficiency" or "replacement"

You don't need a "Chief AI Officer" to lead this. You need **leaders across the business who care about people as much as process.**

Final Thought: Retraining Is Cheaper Than Losing Trust

AI may cut costs. But if it destroys trust, erases institutional knowledge, and turns your workforce into passengers instead of partners — the long-term cost is steep.

Investing in retraining isn't charity. It's **continuity insurance.** It ensures that the people who know your business best can evolve with it — not be left behind.

And for customers, employees, and partners watching your every move, it sends the clearest possible message:

We don't just automate. We adapt — together.

CHAPTER 7

The Ethics Battlefield

Who Decides What's "Right" for AI?

Artificial intelligence is transforming how decisions are made — in hiring, lending, policing, healthcare, education, and beyond. But as machines take on responsibilities once reserved for people, a pressing question emerges: **Who decides what AI should do, and what it *shouldn't*?**

This question isn't theoretical. Every AI system reflects a set of embedded values — from what data it's trained on, to what outcomes it optimizes, to what behaviors it rewards or punishes. These aren't neutral choices. They're moral, cultural, and political judgments — often made behind closed doors, by a small group of developers, data scientists, or executives.

The problem is simple: **AI systems make decisions that impact real people, but most people have no say in how those systems are built.**

In a machine-driven society, determining what's "right" is no longer just a question for ethicists or regulators. It's a boardroom issue, a product issue, and increasingly, **a public trust issue.**

Why "Ethics" in AI Can't Be Left to the Engineers

AI development often moves faster than organizational oversight. Teams optimize for performance, cost, or speed — without pausing to ask: "Should we build this?" or "Who could be harmed by this?"

When ethics are treated as an afterthought — or worse, a PR shield — the result is predictable: bias, abuse, and public backlash.

Real consequences of poor ethical oversight:

- Hiring tools that discriminate against women or minorities
- Predictive policing systems that reinforce racial profiling
- Chatbots that spew offensive content or misinformation
- Health algorithms that deprioritize care for certain demographics
- Educational software that penalizes non-standard learning styles

None of these outcomes were *intended.* But they were **enabled —
by teams that didn't ask the right ethical questions, or didn't
have the authority to act on them.**

Real-World Example: Facial Recognition Deployed Without Consent

What Happened
A city government partnered with a private vendor to deploy facial
recognition cameras in public housing, with the goal of reducing
crime. Residents were never consulted. The system was rolled out
quietly, trained on generic datasets not representative of the local
community.

What Went Wrong
The system produced false matches, particularly for Black and
Latino residents. Several individuals were wrongly flagged or
questioned. Civil liberties groups sued. Trust in law enforcement
collapsed.

What We Learn
When technology is deployed without public consent — and
optimized without ethical alignment — it can **erode trust faster
than it builds safety.** Ethics isn't just about intent. It's about
inclusive design, accountability, and transparency.

The Power Hierarchy Behind AI "Values"

At every stage of AI development, someone makes value-based decisions. But the question is: **who gets a seat at the table?**

Key decision-makers in AI ethics (and where risk concentrates):

Role	Power They Hold	Risks Without Oversight
Data Scientists	Choose training data and labeling criteria	Encode bias, exclude populations
Developers	Set model goals and parameters	Optimize for speed or scale, not fairness
Product Managers	Define what "success" looks like	Prioritize engagement over well-being
Executives	Approve funding and market fit	Ignore long-term social risk for short-term gain
Legal/Compliance	Ensure regulatory alignment	Focus on legality, not morality
End Users	Interact with AI outputs	Often powerless to challenge or appeal

If ethical decisions are confined to the technical team — or worse, outsourced to external consultants with no authority — **ethical failure becomes inevitable.**

Why Consensus on "Right" Is So Difficult

Ethics is messy. What's "right" in one culture may not be acceptable in another. AI systems deployed globally can't assume a universal value set — and yet, they often do.

Challenges in defining ethical AI:

- Competing values (e.g., privacy vs. personalization)
- Varying norms across cultures, industries, and demographics
- Lack of formal training in ethics among technical teams
- Business pressure to deploy fast, not reflect deeply
- Legal compliance mistaken for ethical sufficiency
- Power imbalances between designers and users

As AI takes on more human-like roles — making recommendations, judgments, and even predictions — the absence of diverse, informed ethical governance becomes a form of risk.

Tactical Strategies: Embedding Ethics into Decision-Making

Rather than trying to define a universal "right," smart organizations focus on **ethical process** — creating structures that ensure values are considered, risks are surfaced, and decisions are made intentionally.

1. Establish an Internal AI Ethics Board

- Cross-functional team (legal, product, engineering, DEI, executive sponsor)
- Reviews all high-impact AI deployments
- Has veto or escalation power
- Meets quarterly with documented decisions

2. Adopt a Public Ethical Framework

- Use established principles (e.g., OECD AI Principles, Montreal Declaration, IEEE Ethically Aligned Design)
- Publish your organization's commitments (e.g., fairness, explainability, non-discrimination)
- Embed these principles into product planning and vendor procurement

3. Conduct Ethical Impact Assessments

- Before deploying new AI systems, ask:
  - ☐ Who benefits?
  - ☐ Who might be harmed?
  - ☐ What data is being used — and who is missing from it?
  - ☐ What decisions are being automated, and why?
  - ☐ Can users contest or understand outcomes?
- Require this as part of product and procurement review

4. Include Stakeholders in Design

- Involve affected communities in pilot testing and feedback
- Provide opt-out or human override options
- Use surveys, interviews, and user panels for high-impact use cases
- Document changes made in response to stakeholder concerns

5. Make Ethical Performance a KPI

- Track metrics like complaint volume, appeals, user trust, and fairness audits
- Tie executive compensation or product success to ethical benchmarks
- Conduct annual reviews of ethical incidents and responses

For SMBs: What's Possible Without a Full Ethics Team

You don't need a formal "AI ethics department" to act responsibly. Even small businesses can take meaningful steps:

- Use third-party bias checkers and fairness audit tools (many are free or open-source)
- Require vendors to disclose their ethical practices and data governance policies

- Keep a "human in the loop" for all decisions that impact people's rights or access
- Create a code of AI conduct shared with employees and customers
- Don't deploy models you can't explain — if you don't understand it, don't automate it

Ethical maturity is scalable — what matters is **intentionality and consistency.**

Final Thought: Shared Decisions Require Shared Responsibility

No one person should decide what's "right" for AI. Not the CEO. Not the engineer. Not the regulator. But when no one decides — or when decisions are made in silence — harm becomes inevitable.

Ethics must be collective, visible, and enforceable.

The future of AI doesn't need to be perfectly ethical. It needs to be **accountably human** — where decisions reflect diverse values, mistakes are acknowledged, and systems are designed not just to perform, but to serve.

Algorithmic Discrimination and Social Bias

AI systems don't operate in a vacuum. They learn from the world as it is — which means they inherit the world's flaws, prejudices, and inequities. When those systems are deployed at scale, they don't just reflect bias. They **amplify it** — turning subtle inequalities into widespread discrimination.

This is algorithmic bias: when automated systems treat people unfairly based on race, gender, age, disability, or other protected characteristics. It's not always intentional. But it's always impactful — especially when those decisions are invisible, unaccountable, or assumed to be objective just because a machine made them.

For SMBs, enterprises, and public institutions alike, this isn't a theoretical risk. It's a **compliance hazard, a reputational landmine, and a human rights issue**. Whether you're using AI to screen job applicants, evaluate credit risk, personalize marketing, or automate pricing — you're responsible for the outcomes, **biased or not**.

How Bias Enters AI Systems

Bias can enter at every stage of the AI lifecycle — and once it's in, it's hard to detect unless you're looking for it deliberately.

1. Biased Training Data
If a model learns from historical data that's already biased (e.g., hiring records that favored men), it will replicate those patterns — or even optimize for them.

2. Incomplete or Skewed Datasets
Models trained primarily on white, English-speaking, urban, or affluent populations perform poorly on everyone else — often misclassifying or marginalizing them.

3. Labeling Assumptions
Humans label data with their own mental models — often encoding unconscious bias (e.g., labeling assertive speech as "aggressive" only in women or minorities).

4. Proxy Variables
Algorithms may exclude race or gender explicitly, but use proxies like ZIP code, name, or internet behavior that correlate strongly with protected characteristics.

5. Feedback Loops

When biased outcomes shape future inputs (e.g., arrest data feeding predictive policing), the system reinforces and deepens injustice over time.

AI doesn't see race, gender, or class — but it **learns their consequences** unless we design carefully against them.

Real-World Example: AI Recruiting Tool Downgrades Women

What Happened
A global tech company developed an internal AI tool to screen job applicants. The system was trained on ten years of hiring data — which heavily favored male applicants for technical roles.

What Went Wrong
The AI model learned that resumes mentioning "women's organizations," women's colleges, or feminine first names were less likely to be hired. It began automatically downgrading female candidates — despite having no explicit gender field.

What We Learn
Bias doesn't need to be deliberate to be harmful. By trusting historical patterns, the system learned to **replicate systemic discrimination** — invisibly and at scale.

Where Algorithmic Bias Shows Up in Business

Bias isn't limited to big tech. It can show up in the tools SMBs and enterprises use every day — often embedded in off-the-shelf platforms.

High-risk use cases where algorithmic bias is common:

- **Hiring & HR**: Resume screening, video interviews, performance scoring
- **Lending & Finance**: Credit risk models, loan approvals, fraud detection
- **Healthcare**: Diagnosis prediction, treatment recommendation, triage prioritization
- **Marketing**: Ad targeting, personalization, exclusion lists
- **Retail & E-commerce**: Dynamic pricing, product recommendations
- **Education**: Admissions algorithms, student risk scoring
- **Insurance**: Risk-based pricing, claim fraud analysis
- **Public Services**: Benefit eligibility, criminal risk assessment, resource allocation

In these domains, a biased model can do more than make mistakes — it can **systematically deny opportunity** to entire groups.

Legal and Regulatory Exposure

Algorithmic bias isn't just an ethical issue. It's a legal one. Businesses that deploy discriminatory systems — even inadvertently — can face:

- **Civil rights lawsuits** under anti-discrimination laws
- **Regulatory penalties** from the FTC, EEOC, CFPB, or state AGs
- **Contract losses** for failing to meet fairness or DEI commitments
- **Public backlash** from biased outcomes going viral
- **Audits and consent decrees** mandating model retraining or discontinuation

U.S. law does not yet regulate AI directly — but **existing laws still apply**. If your model discriminates, your company is still liable.

Tactical Best Practices: Detecting and Preventing Algorithmic Bias

Fairness isn't guaranteed by intention — it requires process, testing, and governance.

Checklist: Bias Mitigation Across the AI Lifecycle

1. Data Collection
☐ Audit training data for representation across race, gender, age, ability, geography
☐ Avoid historical data that reflects biased hiring, lending, or criminal practices
☐ Engage subject-matter experts and affected communities in dataset design

2. Feature Selection
☐ Remove proxy variables that correlate with protected classes (e.g., ZIP code, alma mater)
☐ Test model sensitivity to demographic shifts — are outputs consistent across groups?

3. Model Training
☐ Use fairness-aware algorithms (e.g., adversarial debiasing, reweighting)
☐ Monitor disparate impact metrics — do different groups get different outcomes?
☐ Include fairness as an optimization goal, not just accuracy

4. Testing and Evaluation
☐ Run pre-deployment bias tests with synthetic and edge-case data
☐ Conduct subgroup analysis — how does performance vary across different user groups?
☐ Involve diverse user testers in pilot evaluations

5. Deployment
☐ Provide explanations for decisions in plain language
☐ Offer appeals or human review for high-stakes outcomes
☐ Log and monitor outcomes for bias drift over time

6. Governance
☐ Establish internal audit routines for fairness and accountability
☐ Require vendors to disclose training data sources and fairness testing results
☐ Include ethical review in product launch gates or risk committees

Bias can't be eliminated entirely. But it can be **measured, managed, and mitigated.**

Inclusive Design Matters

One of the most effective ways to reduce bias is to **involve more perspectives in the design process.** When teams are homogeneous — culturally, racially, professionally — blind spots multiply.

Best practices for inclusive AI design:

- Hire and empower diverse voices across teams — not just for optics, but for impact
- Pay community experts to test and critique your tools
- Include disability advocates in interface and decision-flow reviews
- Make inclusivity a performance goal for product teams
- Track who's being left out — not just who's being served

The more diverse your inputs, the fairer your outcomes.

Final Thought: Bias Is Not Just a Bug — It's a Mirror

Algorithmic bias doesn't come from malicious intent. It comes from letting systems learn from **an unjust world** — without checks, context, or conscience.

AI doesn't fix human bias. It **scales** it.

That's why organizations must treat bias not just as a technical problem, but as a **strategic imperative**. Fairness is not only the right thing to pursue — it's how you earn trust, meet regulation, and build products that serve *everyone*.

Manipulation Through Personalized AI Persuasion

For decades, marketing has relied on personalization: segmenting customers by age, location, or buying behavior to deliver messages that resonate. With AI, personalization has become something much more powerful — and more dangerous. Instead of broad audience segments, AI can now **target individuals at a psychological level, adapting its persuasion in real time based on your behavior, emotions, and vulnerabilities.**

This goes beyond advertising. AI-powered persuasion systems are now shaping how people vote, what news they trust, what products they buy, and even how they feel about themselves. The line between helpful personalization and manipulative exploitation is blurring — and the implications for both business and society are profound.

What Makes AI Persuasion Different

Traditional persuasion requires a human communicator — a salesperson, a marketer, a teacher. AI changes the scale, precision, and persistence of influence.

AI persuasion is different because it is:

- **Hyper-personalized**: AI analyzes your clicks, pauses, tone of voice, and micro-expressions to craft messages tailored only to you.
- **Real-time adaptive**: Unlike static campaigns, AI modifies its approach continuously as it learns what works.
- **Emotionally intelligent**: Sentiment analysis and voice recognition allow systems to detect when you're angry, sad, or excited — and adjust accordingly.
- **Invisible**: Most people don't realize when an AI is persuading them — which makes resistance harder.
- **Scalable**: What a human salesperson could do for 10 people, AI can now do for 10 million simultaneously.

This combination makes AI persuasion a powerful commercial tool — but also a vector for manipulation.

Real-World Example: Political Microtargeting on Social Platforms

What Happened
During recent election cycles, political campaigns used AI-driven ad platforms to microtarget voters. These systems didn't just segment audiences by demographics. They used personal browsing histories, likes, and behavioral cues to identify psychological triggers for each individual.

What Went Wrong
Some voters were bombarded with fear-based ads designed to suppress turnout. Others received overly optimistic messages to inspire action. The same candidate was presented in completely different ways depending on the recipient's vulnerabilities.

What We Learn
AI persuasion doesn't just "sell ideas." It can **distort democracy itself** by delivering invisible, customized realities that no two citizens share. When persuasion is invisible, accountability disappears.

Everyday Manipulation: Not Just Politics

You don't need to be running a national campaign to see AI persuasion in action. It already surrounds consumers every day.

- **E-commerce**: Recommendation engines nudge shoppers toward impulse buys by analyzing browsing time and "hesitation moments."
- **Social media**: Feeds are optimized for outrage or joy to maximize engagement — not truth or well-being.
- **Streaming platforms**: AI suggests what to watch next, steering culture and taste through predicted binge behaviors.
- **Fitness and health apps**: Gamification nudges users into longer streaks, often prioritizing app usage over actual health.
- **Dating apps**: Algorithms manipulate match suggestions to keep users swiping, rather than finding connection quickly.
- **Voice assistants**: Conversational AI can cross-sell or upsell products under the guise of helpfulness.

The danger isn't personalization itself — it's when personalization crosses into **exploitation of human psychology without awareness or consent.**

Why AI Persuasion Works So Well

Humans are naturally susceptible to influence. But AI leverages specific psychological weaknesses at scale.

- **Confirmation bias**: Feeding users content that reinforces existing beliefs.
- **Loss aversion**: Highlighting what people might "miss out on" to drive decisions.
- **Social proof**: Emphasizing that "people like you" chose the same product.
- **Emotional priming**: Using tone, imagery, or music that matches (or manipulates) current mood.
- **Micro-targeted vulnerability**: Exploiting life stages (e.g., divorce, grief, financial strain) detected from digital footprints.

The result: persuasion that doesn't just work **better** — it works **before you even realize you're being persuaded.**

Risks to Businesses and Society

AI persuasion can create short-term profit but long-term damage if abused.

For Businesses:

- Customer backlash if manipulation is exposed.
- Loss of brand trust from opaque targeting practices.
- Regulatory fines for deceptive marketing.
- Over-optimization that drives churn (e.g., customers who feel tricked, not served).

For Society:

- Political polarization fueled by algorithmic echo chambers.
- Erosion of shared reality — everyone sees a different "truth."
- Exploitation of vulnerable populations (e.g., children, elderly, financially insecure).
- Decline of informed consent — people don't realize they're being nudged.
- Normalization of surveillance as a prerequisite for participation in digital life.

When persuasion is invisible, it's indistinguishable from manipulation.

Tactical Safeguards for Responsible Use

AI persuasion doesn't have to be manipulative. It can be used responsibly to align with customer needs and enhance decision-making — if organizations commit to transparency and ethics.

Best Practices for Ethical AI Persuasion:

- **Transparency**: Disclose when AI is influencing recommendations or offers.
- **Consent**: Allow users to opt out of hyper-personalized targeting.
- **Boundaries**: Set red lines — no persuasion based on sensitive attributes (health, religion, politics).
- **Explainability**: Offer plain-language explanations: "We suggested this because…"
- **Oversight**: Establish internal review boards for high-risk persuasion campaigns.
- **Empowerment**: Design nudges that genuinely serve users' interests (e.g., reminders to save, not overspend).
- **Audit Trails**: Log what persuasion strategies were used, and measure outcomes for fairness.

Executive Checklist:

☐ Can we explain how our AI chooses what to show a customer?
☐ Would customers be comfortable if they knew how persuasion works?
☐ Are we optimizing for long-term trust, or just short-term conversions?
☐ Do we have safeguards for vulnerable populations (children, elderly)?
☐ Could this tactic cause reputational damage if exposed publicly?

Final Thought: Influence Is Inevitable — But Exploitation Is a Choice

AI will always persuade. That's what it does: optimize decisions, recommend content, guide actions. The real question is whether persuasion is **aligned with human well-being** or simply with corporate goals.

Leaders must recognize that **trust is the currency of the machine age.** Customers, employees, and citizens will forgive mistakes — but not manipulation. The organizations that win in the AI era will be those that **persuade transparently, serve authentically, and respect human agency above all else.**

The Moral Questions Around Autonomous Weapons

Few applications of artificial intelligence generate as much ethical urgency as autonomous weapons. Unlike other AI systems — which recommend, predict, or automate business processes — autonomous weapons hold the power to make **life-and-death decisions** without direct human intervention.

Military leaders see them as force multipliers: faster response times, reduced risk to soldiers, and tactical superiority. But the deeper question is not about strategy. It's about morality.

Should machines be allowed to decide who lives and who dies?

That question sits at the heart of international debates, military policy discussions, and human rights advocacy. The answers — or lack of them — will shape not just the future of warfare, but the future of accountability, law, and human dignity.

Why Autonomous Weapons Raise Unique Ethical Concerns

Autonomous weapons, often referred to as **lethal autonomous weapon systems (LAWS)**, differ from traditional weapons in one fundamental way: they shift decision-making from humans to machines.

This creates several moral flashpoints:

- **Loss of human judgment**: Decisions about lethal force traditionally require human deliberation, context, and moral reasoning. Machines optimize for efficiency, not ethics.
- **Accountability gaps**: If an autonomous drone commits a war crime, who is responsible — the programmer, the commander, or the algorithm itself?
- **Dehumanization of conflict**: Removing humans from combat lowers the emotional and ethical barriers to killing.
- **Unpredictable escalation**: Algorithms may misinterpret intent, causing accidental attacks that spiral into broader conflict.
- **Targeting civilians**: AI systems trained on imperfect data can misclassify civilians, infrastructure, or aid workers as threats.

In short: autonomy in weapons doesn't just change tactics. It changes the **moral fabric of warfare.**

Real-World Example: Drone Strikes With Minimal Human Oversight

What Happened
Reports from conflict zones indicate that AI-powered drones have been deployed to track, select, and attack targets with limited human supervision. In some documented cases, these systems relied on pattern recognition — such as identifying "suspicious movement" or "military-age males" — to initiate strikes.

What Went Wrong
Errors in target identification led to civilian casualties, including aid workers and children. The reviewing chain of command assumed the AI system's analysis was reliable, reducing human intervention in final decisions.

What We Learn
The "automation bias" — the human tendency to trust machine outputs — magnifies the risk of wrongful deaths when autonomous weapons are used. The lack of transparency and accountability leaves victims without justice, and operators without responsibility.

The Core Moral Questions

1. Should Machines Have the Right to Kill?
Many ethicists argue that lethal decisions inherently require human conscience, empathy, and proportionality — qualities machines cannot replicate.

2. Can Algorithmic Warfare Ever Be Fair?
Even if machines could reduce some human errors, they cannot ensure compliance with humanitarian principles like distinction (combatants vs. civilians) or proportionality (force vs. necessity).

3. Who Bears Responsibility?

When outcomes go wrong, assigning blame is nearly impossible. Was it the coder? The manufacturer? The military leader who deployed it? This "accountability vacuum" undermines justice.

4. Will Autonomy Lower the Threshold for War?

If leaders can fight wars without risking their own soldiers, they may be more willing to engage in conflict, increasing global instability.

5. How Do We Prevent an Arms Race?

If one nation deploys autonomous weapons, others may feel compelled to follow, leading to destabilization and proliferation — much like nuclear weapons, but harder to control.

International Debate and Regulatory Gaps

- **United Nations**: Multiple efforts have been made under the UN Convention on Certain Conventional Weapons (CCW) to restrict or ban lethal autonomous weapons, but consensus is lacking.
- **European Union**: Some members advocate for a binding treaty banning LAWS.
- **United States & China**: Both invest heavily in military AI, arguing that existing international law is sufficient.
- **Human Rights Groups**: Organizations like the Campaign to Stop Killer Robots argue for a preemptive ban, citing moral and humanitarian grounds.

The lack of global consensus creates a dangerous vacuum. While nations debate definitions, technology continues to advance and proliferate.

Tactical Considerations for Businesses and Governments

Even for organizations outside defense, the rise of autonomous weapons poses indirect risks. Defense contractors, technology providers, and even civilian AI firms may find their innovations repurposed for military use.

Best Practices for Ethical Guardrails:

- **Due Diligence**: Audit partnerships and contracts to ensure technologies aren't misapplied to lethal autonomy.
- **Ethical Clauses**: Include restrictions in licensing agreements prohibiting use in autonomous weapons.
- **Transparency**: Disclose how AI research could be dual-use and what safeguards are in place.
- **Public Engagement**: Involve stakeholders in policy setting, especially for companies working on vision, robotics, or decision systems.
- **Support Regulation**: Advocate for international agreements that keep humans in the loop for lethal decisions.

Final Thought: The Human Line We Cannot Cross

AI can enhance logistics, reconnaissance, and defense. But when it comes to lethal force, **outsourcing morality to machines is a line humanity may regret crossing.** The decision to take a life must remain a profoundly human responsibility — informed by law, conscience, and accountability.

The moral question is not whether autonomous weapons *can* be built. They already exist. The moral question is whether we, as societies, will allow them to decide matters of life and death.

Building Ethical Frameworks Everyone Can Trust

Trust in artificial intelligence doesn't come from clever marketing, regulatory fine print, or technical jargon. It comes from visible, consistent frameworks that prove an organization is committed to fairness, accountability, and transparency. In a world where AI touches hiring, healthcare, finance, and even democracy, businesses cannot afford to treat ethics as an afterthought. They need clear, actionable structures that make ethical principles part of everyday operations.

Why Frameworks Matter More Than Promises

Many companies issue public statements about responsible AI. But without frameworks that define how decisions are made, who reviews them, and what recourse exists when things go wrong, those statements collapse under scrutiny. A trusted framework provides clarity on three levels: it sets standards for behavior, it enforces accountability, and it creates transparency for employees, customers, and regulators alike. Without it, ethical commitments remain slogans, not safeguards.

Real-World Example: Healthcare AI with an Ethics Council

What Happened

A hospital system implemented an AI tool to predict patient readmissions. Before deployment, leadership formed an internal ethics council including clinicians, legal staff, IT security, and patient advocates. The council reviewed training data, testing processes, and appeal procedures for flagged patients.

What Went Right

By embedding diverse voices into the decision-making process, the hospital identified gaps in data that could have disadvantaged patients from rural areas. They adjusted the model and implemented a patient appeals process. Trust in the system increased, and staff reported more confidence using the tool.

What We Learn

Frameworks grounded in inclusion and oversight prevent harm and build legitimacy. Ethics isn't about slowing progress — it's about building solutions that last.

Components of a Trusted Ethical Framework

To be credible, an AI ethics framework must go beyond principles. It needs structure, accountability, and accessibility.

Core components include:

- Clear guiding principles such as fairness, transparency, privacy, and human oversight
- A cross-functional ethics committee with decision-making authority
- Processes for risk assessment before deployment of new AI systems

- Documentation and audit requirements for data sources, model training, and outcomes
- Transparency channels for employees, customers, and regulators
- Mechanisms for appeal or contesting automated decisions
- Continuous monitoring for bias, drift, and unintended consequences

How SMBs Can Build Ethical Frameworks Without Heavy Overhead

Small and mid-sized businesses may not have dedicated ethics teams, but they can still implement lightweight frameworks that scale with their needs.

Practical steps include:

- Assigning responsibility for AI ethics to an existing risk or compliance officer
- Adopting published frameworks like the OECD AI Principles as a baseline
- Building a simple risk review checklist for each new AI tool or vendor
- Conducting annual audits of AI use across the business
- Publishing a short, plain-language AI use policy for customers and employees
- Joining industry consortiums or local groups working on AI ethics standards

The Business Benefits of Getting This Right

Strong ethical frameworks are not just defensive measures. They create strategic advantages. Companies that demonstrate responsible AI practices attract more trust from customers, retain employees who value accountability, and reduce the risk of regulatory fines or lawsuits. Most importantly, they build resilience by avoiding the kind of reputational damage that can cripple a business overnight when AI goes wrong.

Final Thought: Ethics as Infrastructure

In the age of machine-driven decisions, ethics is not a marketing layer or a compliance hurdle. It is infrastructure. Just as cybersecurity and data governance became board-level priorities, AI ethics must be woven into the fabric of every organization. A trusted framework turns principles into practice — ensuring that as businesses innovate with AI, they do so in a way that protects people, preserves dignity, and sustains long-term trust.

CHAPTER 8

Building a Culture of AI Safety

Moving from Reactive to Proactive Risk Management

Most organizations discover the risks of AI the hard way — after a bias incident, a data breach, a compliance violation, or a public backlash. That is **reactive risk management**: responding once harm has already occurred. In an AI-driven economy, this approach is far too costly. The speed, scale, and opacity of machine learning mean problems multiply faster than humans can contain them. By the time you notice an issue, the damage — to customers, reputation, or revenue — may already be irreversible.

Proactive risk management shifts the mindset. Instead of waiting for problems, organizations anticipate them. Instead of patching failures, they build guardrails before deployment. Instead of siloed reactions, they embed oversight into every stage of the AI lifecycle. Proactivity requires more upfront work, but it pays off in reduced crises, stronger trust, and smoother adoption.

Why Proactive Management Matters in AI

Unlike traditional IT risks, AI risks are dynamic. Models evolve as they learn. Data changes over time. Behaviors shift depending on context. This makes AI inherently harder to control once released into production. Relying on reactive governance creates three critical vulnerabilities:

- **Hidden Bias Amplification**: A model may run for months before leaders realize it disadvantages certain groups. By then, legal and reputational damage has set in.
- **Silent Data Drift**: An AI system may gradually degrade in accuracy as data inputs shift. If no monitoring is in place, poor decisions accumulate undetected.

- **Compounded Costs**: Fixing AI problems post-deployment requires retraining, rebuilding, or litigation — all far more expensive than early prevention.

Proactive strategies acknowledge these dynamics and design safety into the process.

Real-World Example: Financial Institution's AI Audit Program

What Happened
A mid-sized bank introduced AI for loan approvals. To avoid regulatory blowback, leadership mandated quarterly bias and accuracy audits before the system launched. Independent reviewers tested outputs against different demographic groups and monitored performance over time.

What Went Right
The audits uncovered disparities early, allowing the bank to recalibrate its model before it went live. They also established monitoring dashboards for ongoing performance. When regulators later reviewed the program, the bank had documentation showing proactive oversight.

What We Learn
Embedding proactive checks not only reduced risk but also **increased trust with regulators and customers.** The bank avoided reputational fallout and positioned itself as a responsible innovator.

Building a Proactive Risk Posture

Shifting from reaction to prevention requires organizational discipline. It's not about slowing innovation — it's about ensuring resilience and sustainability.

Steps to move toward proactive risk management:

1. **Risk Mapping Before Deployment**
   Identify potential harms (bias, privacy, misuse) before building or buying an AI system. Document how these risks could materialize and who would be affected.
2. **Pre-Deployment Testing**
   Run simulations and audits with diverse datasets and edge cases. Test not just for accuracy, but for fairness, explainability, and resilience.
3. **Ongoing Monitoring and Alerts**
   Set thresholds for acceptable error rates or bias indicators. Deploy monitoring dashboards that trigger alerts when models drift from safe boundaries.
4. **Governance Checkpoints**
   Require formal review and sign-off before an AI tool is launched, updated, or integrated into sensitive workflows.
5. **Scenario Planning**
   Develop playbooks for what to do if the system fails — including communication protocols, human fallback options, and remediation strategies.
6. **Stakeholder Involvement**
   Engage employees, customers, and external experts early to identify blind spots. Proactive risk management depends on diverse perspectives.

Executive Checklist for Proactivity

☐ Have we conducted an AI impact assessment before rollout?

☐ Do we have ongoing monitoring in place for accuracy, bias, and drift?

☐ Can employees or customers appeal AI-driven decisions easily?

☐ Do we have a playbook for AI failure scenarios?

☐ Are vendors required to disclose their data sources and risk mitigation steps?

☐ Does leadership receive regular reporting on AI performance and risks?

From Compliance to Competitive Advantage

Proactive risk management isn't just about avoiding disasters. It can also be a source of competitive strength. Companies that build risk awareness into their AI strategy:

- Earn faster regulatory approval and lighter audits
- Gain customer trust by demonstrating accountability
- Prevent costly recalls, retraining, and litigation
- Empower teams to innovate confidently within clear guardrails
- Build resilience against reputational shocks

In the long run, proactive organizations don't just avoid failure. They **create safer, stronger foundations for growth.**

Final Thought: Lead the Risk, Don't Chase It

Reactive governance assumes problems are inevitable. Proactive governance assumes responsibility for preventing them. In the AI era, this distinction determines not just whether you avoid crises, but whether your organization earns the trust to keep innovating.

Businesses that shift from reaction to anticipation will define the future of AI — not as a risk to be feared, but as a tool to be trusted.

The Role of Transparency and Explainability

Artificial intelligence thrives on complexity. Neural networks with billions of parameters can generate predictions, recommendations, and decisions at speeds no human could match. But with that complexity comes opacity. Too often, businesses and individuals are asked to accept AI's conclusions without understanding how they were reached. That's where transparency and explainability become essential — not just as technical features, but as foundations of trust.

Transparency and explainability ensure that AI is not a "black box" but a system that people can understand, evaluate, and, when necessary, challenge. Without them, organizations risk alienating customers, regulators, and employees alike, while exposing themselves to legal, ethical, and reputational hazards.

Why Transparency Matters

Transparency is about openness: clearly communicating how an AI system works, what data it uses, what it optimizes for, and what its limitations are. In practice, this means making sure that stakeholders

— from employees to regulators to customers — aren't left in the dark about how decisions are made.

Key benefits of transparency:

- **Trust**: Users and customers are more likely to adopt AI tools if they feel informed.
- **Accountability**: Transparency makes it easier to trace responsibility when errors occur.
- **Compliance**: Regulators increasingly require disclosures about AI's operation and impact.
- **Fairness**: Transparency helps surface hidden biases or blind spots in data and models.

Without transparency, AI becomes a liability. With it, AI becomes a tool that people can engage with responsibly.

Why Explainability Matters

Explainability is the next step: providing understandable reasons for AI-driven decisions. An AI doesn't need to reveal every parameter in its model — but it does need to show enough for humans to grasp the logic.

For example:

- A bank applicant denied a loan should know if it was due to credit history, income level, or spending patterns — not an opaque algorithm.
- A patient affected by an AI medical recommendation should understand what risk factors triggered the outcome.
- An employee evaluated by a performance model should see what data influenced the result.

Explainability doesn't just support trust. It supports **agency.** People deserve the ability to respond, appeal, or correct mistakes when AI makes decisions about their lives.

Real-World Example: Credit Scoring Transparency

What Happened
A fintech startup launched an AI-driven credit scoring tool aimed at underserved populations. Early adoption was strong — until customers began complaining that their scores were lower than expected, with no explanation provided.

What Went Wrong
Because the system offered no explainability, applicants couldn't challenge errors or understand why they were being denied. Regulators intervened, forcing the company to suspend the product until it implemented clear disclosure policies.

What We Learn
Even well-intentioned AI systems can fail without explainability. For customers, a score without a reason isn't just unhelpful — it feels arbitrary, unfair, and dehumanizing.

Balancing Opacity and Clarity

Not all AI models are easily explainable. Deep learning systems, in particular, often involve trade-offs between performance and interpretability. But organizations can strike a balance by combining technical tools with plain-language communication.

Techniques include:

- **Model interpretability tools** such as SHAP, LIME, and counterfactual explanations
- **Feature importance scoring** to show which inputs matter most
- **Simplified surrogate models** that approximate complex systems for human review

- **User-facing explanations** written in clear, non-technical language

The goal isn't to open every line of code. It's to provide enough clarity that stakeholders understand the basis of decisions and can act accordingly.

Practical Steps for Businesses

To embed transparency and explainability into AI governance, organizations should adopt concrete practices:

- ☐ Publish plain-language summaries of how AI systems are used in your business
- ☐ Provide user-level explanations for significant decisions (loans, hiring, benefits)
- ☐ Require vendors to disclose training data sources and model limitations
- ☐ Audit systems regularly for interpretability and bias outcomes
- ☐ Create internal policies that prohibit deploying black-box models in high-stakes domains
- ☐ Train employees to explain AI outputs to customers, regulators, and peers

For SMBs especially, building explainability into vendor selection is key. If a provider can't explain how their tool works, you should question whether it's safe to deploy.

The Business Payoff of Openness

Transparency and explainability are sometimes seen as friction — slowing innovation or complicating deployment. In reality, they are accelerators. They build customer trust, reduce regulatory risk, and create smoother adoption curves. They also differentiate organizations: in a world full of opaque AI, **the company willing to explain itself will stand out as trustworthy.**

Final Thought: Clarity Is the Currency of Trust

AI doesn't have to be a black box. It can be a glass box — powerful, but also understandable. The organizations that lead will be those that treat transparency and explainability not as compliance burdens but as competitive advantages. Because when customers, employees, and regulators can see how decisions are made, they don't just trust the system. They trust you.

Encouraging Whistleblowers and Ethical Oversight

In the fast-moving world of artificial intelligence, the greatest risks often aren't technical flaws — they're cultural silences. Employees, contractors, or partners may see issues first: biased models, unethical use cases, unsafe shortcuts, or privacy violations. Yet too often, those voices are ignored, punished, or forced underground. Without safe channels for whistleblowing, organizations leave themselves blind to emerging dangers until they erupt into full-blown crises.

Encouraging whistleblowers is not about inviting disloyalty. It's about building **a culture of trust where speaking up is a form of protection — for customers, employees, and the business itself.** Paired with structured ethical oversight, this culture becomes a safeguard against both technical and reputational harm.

Why Whistleblowers Are Critical in AI

AI systems are uniquely prone to hidden risks. Models can embed bias, data can be misused, and automation can create harm that leadership never intended. Because AI is complex and often opaque, **those closest to the systems are the ones most likely to spot problems first.**

When employees feel unsafe to speak up, small issues stay buried. When they feel protected, they provide an early warning system that saves the organization from larger failures.

Key benefits of empowering whistleblowers:

- **Early detection of risk** before harm escalates
- **Stronger accountability** for vendors, partners, and executives
- **Alignment with compliance** in heavily regulated industries
- **Cultural resilience** where staff feel ownership over ethical outcomes

Real-World Example: AI Moderation Worker Speaks Out

What Happened
A contract employee tasked with moderating harmful content for an AI training dataset raised concerns about the psychological toll of the work, inadequate pay, and lack of safeguards. When ignored internally, they went public. Media coverage revealed exploitative labor practices behind the company's "automated" content filters.

What Went Wrong
Instead of addressing the concerns early, leadership dismissed them. The backlash damaged the company's reputation, sparked regulatory inquiries, and forced expensive operational overhauls.

What We Learn
Whistleblowers don't create crises — they reveal them.
Organizations that fail to listen internally often end up dealing with far greater external consequences.

Building Structures for Safe Whistleblowing

To make whistleblowing constructive rather than adversarial, businesses must establish clear, safe, and credible reporting channels.

Core elements of a safe whistleblowing program:

- Confidential reporting channels (hotlines, encrypted forms, ombudsman offices)
- Anti-retaliation policies that protect employees from career harm
- Independent review processes, not just internal managers with conflicts of interest
- Regular communication that speaking up is welcomed and valued
- Visible examples of issues raised and addressed transparently

When people know their concerns will be taken seriously — without punishment — they are far more likely to help protect the organization.

The Role of Ethical Oversight

Whistleblowing alone isn't enough. Organizations also need **formal oversight structures** that ensure AI deployments are reviewed, tested, and accountable.

Ethical oversight mechanisms include:

- AI ethics committees that review high-risk projects before launch
- Cross-functional panels (legal, HR, engineering, DEI, external experts)

- Documented processes for bias audits, data reviews, and risk assessments
- Reporting pipelines that escalate unresolved concerns to executive leadership
- External advisory boards or partnerships to provide independent critique

Oversight ensures that problems identified by whistleblowers aren't buried, but systematically investigated and resolved.

Practical Steps for SMBs

Small and mid-sized businesses may not have the resources for full ethics boards, but they can still create meaningful oversight and whistleblower protections.

- Assign responsibility to a designated ethics officer or compliance manager
- Provide a simple, anonymous channel for employees to raise concerns
- Include ethical review questions in vendor and product procurement
- Publish a clear anti-retaliation statement in employee handbooks
- Create quarterly reviews where leadership discusses AI risks openly with staff

These steps signal that ethics is not optional — it's embedded in daily operations.

Executive Checklist

☐ Do we have safe, anonymous channels for reporting AI-related concerns?
☐ Are employees protected from retaliation if they raise issues?
☐ Is there a cross-functional committee overseeing AI deployments?

☐ Do whistleblower reports receive timely and visible follow-up?

☐ Are vendors and contractors held to the same ethical oversight standards?

☐ Does leadership publicly reinforce the value of ethical reporting?

Final Thought: Whistleblowers Are Protectors, Not Enemies

In the machine age, silence is more dangerous than dissent. AI can magnify small risks into systemic harm faster than leaders can react. Whistleblowers are not disloyal; they are the **last line of defense when systems — or leadership — fail to see what's coming.**

When paired with robust ethical oversight, whistleblower protections become more than risk management. They become a statement of values: that your organization prioritizes people, fairness, and accountability over unchecked speed or secrecy.

Collaboration Between Governments, Businesses, and Citizens

The risks and rewards of artificial intelligence extend far beyond any single company, sector, or country. Unlike earlier technologies, AI doesn't just disrupt markets — it redefines **power, privacy, employment, and trust** across society. That makes collaboration essential. No government can regulate AI in isolation, no business can self-police indefinitely, and no citizen can defend their rights without being part of the conversation.

For AI to serve humanity rather than exploit it, **governments, businesses, and citizens must work together** — each bringing unique responsibilities, checks, and contributions to the table.

Why Collaboration Is Non-Negotiable

AI is borderless. Data crosses jurisdictions, platforms, and industries. A flawed model trained in one country can harm citizens in another. A powerful algorithm deployed in finance can ripple into healthcare or education. Without collaboration, the system becomes fragmented — with loopholes for abuse, uneven protections, and declining trust.

The stakes are too high for fragmented responses. When governments act alone, they risk overregulating or underenforcing. When businesses self-regulate, they risk prioritizing speed over safety. When citizens are excluded, their rights and concerns are ignored. Collaboration is the only path to balanced progress.

What Each Stakeholder Brings

Governments

- Set legal boundaries for privacy, safety, and fairness
- Invest in public research and digital literacy programs
- Represent citizens' rights in global negotiations
- Create enforcement mechanisms when things go wrong

Businesses

- Develop and deploy AI systems responsibly
- Maintain transparency about data use and model limitations
- Share best practices across industries
- Invest in ethical innovation rather than shortcuts

Citizens

- Demand accountability and transparency from both business and government
- Provide input on where AI should and shouldn't be deployed
- Participate in democratic processes shaping AI regulation
- Adopt responsible digital habits to reduce exploitation

When these roles are respected and integrated, collaboration creates a cycle of trust.

Real-World Example: EU's AI Act Development

What Happened
The European Union developed the AI Act, the first comprehensive regulatory framework for artificial intelligence. Instead of drafting it solely behind closed doors, EU leaders conducted public consultations, invited businesses to share concerns, and included civil society groups in debates.

What Went Right
The final framework introduced tiered risk categories for AI applications (minimal, limited, high, and unacceptable risk). This balanced innovation with protection, allowing low-risk AI to thrive while restricting systems like mass biometric surveillance.

What We Learn
When governments, businesses, and citizens collaborate, policies are more **nuanced, enforceable, and trusted.** Regulation ceases to be adversarial and becomes a shared safety net.

Practical Paths to Collaboration

Collaboration can feel abstract, but there are concrete ways to make it real.

For Governments:

- Hold public consultations on AI policies
- Fund open-source and public-good AI projects
- Partner with SMBs to ensure compliance is affordable and practical
- Support cross-border coordination on AI safety standards

For Businesses:

- Publish transparent AI use policies for customers and employees
- Participate in multi-stakeholder forums and ethics alliances
- Share anonymized research on bias, safety, and model performance
- Provide AI literacy resources to customers and communities

For Citizens:

- Engage in civic discussions on AI regulation and ethics
- Support organizations advocating for fair AI practices
- Demand plain-language disclosures from companies using AI
- Educate themselves and their families about data rights and AI risks

Executive Checklist for Collaboration

☐ Have we engaged regulators early about our AI systems and their risks?

☐ Are we participating in industry or public forums on AI ethics?

☐ Do our customers know how their data is used — in clear, accessible terms?

☐ Are we contributing to community AI literacy, not just shareholder profit?

☐ Do we treat citizen feedback as valuable input, or as noise to be ignored?

Final Thought: Shared Power, Shared Responsibility

AI will shape the next century as profoundly as electricity or the internet. But unlike those technologies, it raises immediate moral and social questions. Who benefits? Who is left behind? Who decides the rules?

The only sustainable answer is collaboration. Governments must govern with foresight, businesses must innovate with accountability, and citizens must engage with awareness. If any group abdicates its role, AI will tilt toward exploitation. But when all three work together, AI becomes not just a powerful tool — but a shared asset that strengthens economies, protects rights, and enhances human dignity.

Creating a Global Safety Mindset Before It's Too Late

Artificial intelligence is not confined by borders, laws, or cultures. An algorithm trained in one country can be deployed worldwide in a matter of hours. A vulnerability in one system can ripple into another halfway across the globe. A weaponized AI breakthrough in one nation can spark an arms race others feel compelled to join. In this environment, **safety cannot be a local afterthought — it must be a global mindset.**

The world has already learned this lesson with climate change, nuclear proliferation, and financial crises: fragmented responses to global risks lead to uneven protections and systemic failures. With AI, the timeline is even shorter. Systems are evolving faster than regulations, and adversaries are quick to exploit gaps. Waiting until "something goes wrong" is not a strategy.

A global safety mindset means building common standards, shared accountability, and collective vigilance — before the consequences become unmanageable.

Why a Global Safety Approach Is Urgent

Several factors make AI uniquely dangerous to handle piecemeal:

- **Borderless technology**: AI tools, models, and datasets can cross borders instantly, with no customs checks or tariffs.
- **Concentration of power**: A handful of corporations and nations currently control the most powerful AI systems, leaving others dependent and vulnerable.
- **Dual-use nature**: The same algorithm that powers personalized healthcare can also fuel surveillance or cyberattacks.
- **Unintended consequences**: Once AI systems scale, their failures — bias, misinformation, or autonomous errors — spread exponentially.
- **Acceleration curve**: Development outpaces governance. By the time laws catch up, harmful use cases may already be entrenched.

Without a global perspective, countries risk inconsistent protections, regulatory arbitrage, and competitive races to the bottom.

Real-World Example: Deepfake Proliferation

What Happened
Deepfake technology — once confined to research labs — is now widely available through open-source platforms and commercial apps. Within a few years, it spread globally, fueling scams, election interference, and abuse without effective oversight.

What Went Wrong
Because no international standards existed, each nation responded differently. Some banned deepfakes outright, others ignored them, and most still struggle to enforce penalties. The fragmented response allowed bad actors to thrive in jurisdictions with weak controls.

What We Learn

A lack of coordinated global safety measures creates **safe havens for misuse**. By the time regulators act, the harm is already widespread.

Elements of a Global Safety Mindset

Creating shared safety norms does not require identical laws in every country. It requires **common principles and collective responsibility.**

Key elements include:

- **Minimum global standards**: Agreement on baseline safety rules (e.g., transparency, testing, accountability).
- **Cross-border cooperation**: Shared frameworks for data sharing, model evaluation, and crisis response.
- **Ethical consensus**: Recognition of red lines — such as banning fully autonomous lethal weapons or unregulated biometric surveillance.
- **Global monitoring**: Watchdogs that identify risks, share intelligence, and prevent gaps.
- **Public involvement**: Ensuring civil society has a voice in shaping norms, not just governments and corporations.

What Governments, Businesses, and Citizens Can Do

Governments:

- Participate in multilateral agreements, not just national laws.
- Support international watchdogs like the UN, OECD, or new AI safety agencies.
- Fund AI literacy campaigns to prepare citizens for both risks and benefits.

Businesses:

- Commit to ethical codes that apply globally, not just in favorable jurisdictions.
- Share best practices across borders to raise industry-wide safety standards.
- Refuse to exploit regulatory gaps for short-term gain.

Citizens:

- Demand transparency about how AI is used in their lives.
- Support democratic oversight of AI deployment.
- Pressure both governments and businesses to collaborate internationally.

Executive Checklist for Global Safety

☐ Do we align our AI practices with emerging global standards (e.g., OECD, UNESCO, EU AI Act)?

☐ Have we assessed whether our vendors or partners operate in jurisdictions with weak AI safety laws?

☐ Are we preparing for cross-border risks such as supply chain disruption, disinformation, or cyber escalation?

☐ Are we contributing — publicly and visibly — to shared safety initiatives?

☐ Do our leaders understand that AI safety is not only local compliance, but global responsibility?

Final Thought: The Window Is Closing

The world still has a choice. Right now, AI is powerful but not yet fully entrenched. Standards can still be set, cooperation can still be built, and mistakes can still be prevented. But if governments, businesses, and citizens wait until a catastrophic failure — a manipulated election, a runaway autonomous system, or a global financial disruption — it may be too late to course-correct.

Creating a global safety mindset is not about fear. It's about foresight. It is the recognition that intelligence, once unleashed, cannot be put back in the box — but it can be guided. The future of AI will be written not by the fastest adopters, but by those willing to collaborate across borders to ensure that progress does not come at the expense of humanity.

Closing Reflections

Artificial intelligence is no longer a distant promise or a niche experiment — it is shaping decisions, opportunities, and risks in every corner of society. From supply chains and schools to battlefields and boardrooms, AI has already proven itself to be both a force for progress and a catalyst for harm. The choice before us is not whether AI will transform our world, but **how** it will transform it — and who will bear the costs if we ignore its dangers.

Throughout this book, we have seen that the difference between risk and resilience is not technology itself, but leadership. Business owners, policymakers, and citizens cannot afford to be passive consumers of AI. They must be **active stewards** — asking hard questions, setting clear guardrails, and making values-driven decisions about what kind of future they are willing to accept.

If there is one message to carry forward, it is this: AI does not absolve us of responsibility; it demands more of it. The tools we build today will echo across generations. By choosing transparency over secrecy, fairness over convenience, and foresight over reaction, we can ensure that artificial intelligence strengthens our societies instead of undermining them.

The future is not yet written. The power to shape it — wisely, ethically, and humanely — remains in our hands.

Glossary of Terms

Adversarial Attack
A technique used to manipulate AI models by subtly altering inputs (such as images or text) so the system produces incorrect outputs without humans noticing.

Algorithmic Bias
Unfair or discriminatory outcomes produced by AI systems due to biased data, flawed design, or hidden assumptions in algorithms.

Artificial General Intelligence (AGI)
A theoretical form of AI capable of performing any intellectual task a human can, with reasoning, creativity, and adaptability beyond narrow use cases.

Artificial Narrow Intelligence (ANI)
AI designed for specific tasks such as image recognition, language translation, or fraud detection. Current AI systems fall into this category.

Autonomous Weapons Systems (AWS)
Weapons that can identify, select, and engage targets without human intervention, raising serious ethical and legal concerns.

Black Box AI
An AI system whose decision-making process is so complex that even its developers cannot easily explain how outputs are produced.

Chatbot
An AI-powered conversational system that interacts with users via text or voice, commonly used in customer service and virtual assistants.

Computer Vision
A field of AI focused on enabling machines to interpret and analyze visual information from images or video.

Data Drift
The gradual change in model accuracy or reliability due to shifts in input data over time.

Deep Learning
A subset of machine learning that uses multi-layered neural networks to process large datasets and identify complex patterns.

Deepfake
Synthetic media, often video or audio, generated using AI to convincingly mimic real people, frequently exploited for scams or misinformation.

Explainability
The ability to make AI outputs understandable to humans by showing how and why a system made a decision.

Generative AI
AI systems that can create new content such as text, images, audio, or code, based on training data patterns.

Ghost Work
Invisible human labor that supports AI systems, such as labeling training data, moderating content, or reviewing model outputs.

Hallucination (AI)
When a generative AI system produces information that is false or fabricated but presented as factually accurate.

Human-in-the-Loop (HITL)
A design approach that ensures humans remain involved in reviewing or approving AI decisions, especially in high-stakes contexts.

Large Language Model (LLM)
A type of AI trained on vast text datasets to understand and generate human-like language.

Machine Learning (ML)
A branch of AI where systems learn patterns from data and improve performance without being explicitly programmed.

Model Drift
The degradation of AI performance over time as data, conditions, or user behaviors change.

Neural Network
A computational system inspired by the human brain, consisting of layers of nodes that process and transmit information.

Predictive Policing
The use of AI to analyze crime data and predict where crimes are likely to occur, criticized for reinforcing systemic bias.

Reinforcement Learning
A type of machine learning where an AI system learns through trial and error, receiving feedback through rewards or penalties.

Supervised Learning
An ML method where models are trained on labeled datasets with known outputs to learn predictions.

Synthetic Data
Artificially generated data used to train AI systems, often employed to supplement or protect real-world datasets.

Transparency
The principle of making AI processes, data sources, and limitations clear and accessible to stakeholders.

Unsupervised Learning
An ML method where models analyze unlabeled data to find hidden structures or groupings.

Thank you for taking the time to read this Book.

If you found value in this book, I'd be deeply grateful if you took a few minutes of your time to share your feedback. An **honnest review on Amazon**, a personal recommendation to a colleague, or simply applying what you've learned in your work all go a long way. Your encouragement helps fuel future writing, research, and tool development — and inspires continued work.

— Eric LeBouthillier
Founder, AcraSolution

www.ingramcontent.com/pod-product-compliance
Lightning Source LLC
Chambersburg PA
CBHW071202210326
41597CB00016B/1638